The Doctrine
of Man's Impotence

The Doctrine
of Man's Impotence

By

Arthur W. Pink

Printed in the United States of America and Australia.

Bottom of the Hill Publishing
Memphis, TN
www.BottomoftheHillPublishing.com

ISBN: 978-1-61203-324-2

Contents

Chapter 1
Introduction

The title of this second section of our book (Part II from Gleanings from the Scriptures; Man's Total Depravity) may occasion a raising of the eyebrows. That we should designate the spiritual helplessness of fallen man a "doctrine" is likely to cause surprise, for it is certainly not so regarded in most circles today. Yet this is hardly to be wondered at. Didactic preaching has fallen into such general disuse that more than one important doctrine is no longer heard from the pulpits. If on the one hand there is a deplorable lack of a clear and definite portrayal of the character of God, on the other there is also a woeful absence of any lucid and comprehensive presentation of the teaching of Scripture concerning the nature and condition of man. Such failure at either point leads to the most disastrous consequences. A study of this neglected subject is therefore timely and urgent.

Timely and Urgent Study

It is of the utmost importance that people should clearly understand and be made thoroughly aware of their spiritual impotence, for thus alone is a foundation laid for bringing them to see and feel their imperative need of divine grace for salvation. So long as sinners think they have it in their own power to deliver themselves from their death in trespasses and sins, they will never come to Christ that they might have life, for "the whole need not a physician, but they that are sick." So long as people imagine they labor under no insuperable inability to comply with the call of the gospel, they never will be conscious of their entire dependence on Him alone who is able to work in them "all the good pleasure of his goodness, and the work of faith with power" (2 Thess. 1:11). So long as the creature is puffed up with a sense of his own ability to respond to God's requirements, he will never become a suppliant at the footstool of divine mercy.

A careful perusal of what the Word of God has to say on this subject leaves us in no doubt about the awful state of spiritual serfdom into which the fall has brought man. The depravity, blindness and deafness of all mankind in things of a spiritual nature are continually inculcated and emphatically insisted on throughout the Scriptures. Not only is the total inability of the natural man to obtain salvation by deeds of the law frequently asserted, but his utter helplessness in himself to comply with the terms of the gospel is also strongly affirmed—not indirectly and occasionally, but expressly and continually. Both in the Old Testament and in the New, in the declarations of the prophets, of the Lord Christ, and of His apostles, the bondage of the natural man to Satan is often depicted, and his complete impotence to turn to God for deliverance is solemnly and unequivocally set forth. Ignorance or misconception on the matter is therefore inexcusable.

Nevertheless the fact remains that this is a doctrine which is little understood and rarely insisted upon. Notwithstanding the clear and uniform testimony of the Scriptures, the actual conditions of men, their alienation from God, their sinful inability to return to Him, are but feebly apprehended and seldom heard even in orthodox quarters. The fact is that the whole trend of modern thought is in the very opposite direction. For the past century, and increasingly so during the last few decades, the greatness of man—his dignity, his development and his achievements—has been the predominant theme of pulpit and press. The antiscriptural theory of evolution is a blank detail of the fall and its dire consequences, and even where the Darwinian hypothesis has not been accepted, its pernicious influences have been more or less experienced.

The evil effects from the promulgation of the evolutionary lie are far more widespread than most Christians realize. Such a philosophy (if it is entitled to be called that) has induced multitudes of people to suppose that their state is far different from, and vastly superior to, the fearful diagnosis given in Holy Writ. Even among those who have not accepted without considerable reservation the idea that man is slowly but surely progressing, the great majority have been encouraged to believe that their case is far better than it actually is. Consequently, when a servant of God boldly affirms that all the descendants of Adam are so completely enslaved by sin that they are utterly unable to take one step toward Christ for deliverance, he is looked upon as a doleful pessimist or a crazy fanatic. To speak of the spiritual impotence of the natural man is, in our day, to talk in an unknown tongue.

Not only does the appalling ignorance of our generation cause the servant of God to labor under a heavy handicap when seeking to present the scriptural account of man's total inability for good; he is also placed at a serious disadvantage by virtue of the marked distastefulness of this truth. The subject of his moral impotence is far from being a pleasing one to the natural man. He wants to be told that all he needs to do is exert himself, that salvation lies within the power of his will, that he is the determiner of his own destiny. Pride, with its strong dislike of being a debtor to the sovereign grace of God, rises up against it. Self-esteem, with its rabid repugnance of anything which lays the creature in the dust, hotly resents what is so humiliating. Consequently, this truth is either openly rejected or, if seemingly received, is turned to a wrong use.

Moreover, when it is insisted on that man's bondage to sin is both voluntary and culpable, that the guilt for his inability to turn to God or to do anything pleasing in His sight lies at his own door, that his spiritual impotence consists in nothing but the depravity of his own heart and his inveterate enmity against God, then the hatefulness of this doctrine is speedily demonstrated. While men are allowed to think that their spiritual helplessness is involuntary rather than willful, innocent rather than criminal, something to be pitied rather than blamed, they may receive this truth with a measure of toleration; but let them be told that they themselves have forged the shackles which hold them in captivity to sin, that God counts them responsible for the corruption of their hearts, and that their incapability of being holy constitutes the very essence of their guilt, and loud will be their outcries against such a flesh-withering truth.

However repellent this truth may be, it must not be withheld from men. The minister of Christ is not sent forth to please or entertain his congregation, but to declare the counsel of God, and not merely those parts of it which may meet with their approval and acceptance, but "all the counsel of God" (Acts 20:27). If he deliberately omits that which raises their ire, he betrays his trust. Once he starts whittling down his divinely given commission there will be no end to the process, for one class will murmur against this portion of the truth and another against that. The servant of God has nothing to do with the response which is made to his preaching; his business is to deliver the Word of God in its unadulterated purity and leave the results to the One who has called him. And he may be assured at the outset that unless many in his congregation are seriously disturbed by his message, he has failed to deliver it in its clarity.

A Resented Doctrine

No matter how hotly this doctrine of man's spiritual impotence is resented by both the profane and the religious world, it must not be withheld through cowardice. Christ, our supreme Exemplar, announced this truth emphatically and constantly. To the Pharisees He said, "O generation of vipers, how can ye, being evil, speak good things? For out of the abundance of the heart the mouth speaketh" (Matt. 12:34). Men's hearts are so vile, it is utterly impossible that anything holy should issue from them. They can no more change their nature by an effort of will than a leper might heal himself by his own volition. Christ further said, "How can ye believe, which receive honor one of another, and seek not the honor that cometh from God only?" (John 5:44). It is a moral impossibility—pride and humility are opposites. Those who seek to please self and those who sincerely aim at the approbation of God belong to two entirely different stocks.

On another occasion the Lord Christ asked, "Why do ye not understand my speech?" to which He Himself answered, "Even because ye cannot hear my word" (John 8:43). There is no mistaking His meaning here and no evading the force of His solemn utterance. The message of Christ was hateful to their worldly and wicked hearts and could no more be acceptable to them than would wholesome food to birds accustomed to feed on carrion. Man cannot act contrary to his nature; one might as well expect fire to burn downward or water flow upward. "Ye are of your father the devil, and the lusts of your father ye will do" (John 8:44) said the Savior to the Jews. And what was their response? "Say we not well that thou art a Samaritan, and hast a devil?" (v. 48). Sufficient for the servant to be as his Master.

Now if such is the case with the natural man that he can no more break the bonds which hold him in captivity to Satan than he could restore the dead to life, ought he not to be faithfully informed of his wretched condition? If he is so helpless and hopeless in himself that he cannot turn from sin to holiness, that he cannot please God, that he cannot take one step toward Christ for salvation, is it not a kindness to acquaint him with his spiritual impotence, to shatter his dreams of self-sufficiency, to expose the delusion that he is lord of himself? In fact, is it not positively cruel to leave him alone in his complacency and make no effort to bring him face to face with the desperateness of his depravity? Surely anyone with a vestige of charity in his heart will have no difficulty in answering such questions.

It is far from a pleasant task for a physician to tell an unsuspecting patient that his or her heart is organically diseased or to announce to a young person engaging in strenuous activities that his lungs are in such a condition he is totally unfit for violent exertions; nevertheless it is the physician's duty to break such news. Now if this principle holds good in connection with our mortal bodies, how much more so with regard to our never dying spirits. True, there are some doctors who persuade themselves that there are times when it is expedient for them to withhold such information from their patients, but a true physician of souls is never justified in concealing the more distasteful aspect of the truth from those who are under his care. If he is to be free from their blood, he must unsparingly expose the plague of their hearts.

The fact of fallen man's moral inability is indissolubly bound up with the doctrine of his total depravity, and any denial of the one is a repudiation of the other, as any attempt to modify the former is to vitiate the latter. In like manner, the fact of the natural man's impotence to deliver himself from the bondage of sin is inseparably connected with the truth of regeneration; for unless we are without strength in ourselves, what need is there for God to work a miracle of grace in us? It is, then, the reality of the sinner's helplessness which provides the dark background necessary for the gospel, and just in proportion as we are made aware of our helplessness shall we really value the mercy proffered us in the gospel. On the other hand, while we cherish the delusion that we have power to turn to God at any time, just so long we shall continue procrastinating and thereby despise the gracious overtures of the gospel.

William Shedd stated:

A sense of danger excites; a sense of security puts to sleep. A company of gamblers in the sixth story are told that the building is on fire. One of them answers, "We have the key to the fire escape," and all continue the game. Suddenly one exclaims, "The key is lost"; all immediately spring to their feet and endeavor to escape.

Just so long as the sinner believes—because of his erroneous notion of the freedom of his will—that he has the power to repent and believe at any moment, he will defer faith and repentance; he will not so much as beg God to work these graces in him.

The first office of the preacher is to stain the pride of all human glory, to bring down the high looks of man, to make him aware of his sinful perversity, to make him feel that he is unworthy of the least of all God's mercies. His business is to strip him of the rags of his self-righteousness and to shatter his self-sufficiency; to make him conscious of his utter dependence on the mere grace of God. Only he who finds himself absolutely helpless will surrender himself to sovereign grace. Only he who feels himself already sinking under the billows of a justly deserved condemnation will cry out, "Lord, save me, I perish." Only he who has been brought to despair will place the crown of glory on the only head entitled to wear it. Though God alone can make a man conscious of his impotence, He is pleased to use the means of the truth—faithfully dispensed, effectually applied by the Spirit—in doing so.

Chapter 2
Reality

The spiritual impotence of the natural man is no mere product of theological dyspepsia, nor is it a dismal dogma invented during the Dark Ages. It is a solemn fact affirmed by Holy Writ, manifested throughout human history, confirmed in the conscious experience of every genuinely convicted soul. The moral powerlessness of the sinner is not proclaimed in the pulpit today, nor is it believed in by professing Christians generally. When it is insisted that man is so completely the bondslave of sin that he cannot move toward God, the vast majority will regard the statement as utterly unreasonable and reject it with scorn. To tell those who consider themselves to be hale and hearty that they are without strength strikes them as a preposterous assumption unworthy of serious consideration.

Objections of Unbelief
When a servant of God does press this unwelcome truth on his hearers, the fertile mind of unbelief promptly replies with one objection after another. If we are totally devoid of spiritual ability, then assuredly we must be aware of the fact. But that is far from being the case. The skeptic says we are very much aware of our power to do that which is pleasing in God's sight; even though we do not perform it, we could if we would. He also contends that were we so completely the captives of Satan as is declared, we should not be free agents at all. Such a concept as that we will not allow for a moment. Another point of the skeptic is that if man has no power to do that which God requires, then obviously he is not a responsible creature, for he cannot justly be held accountable to do that which is beyond his powers to achieve.

We must establish the fact of man's spiritual impotence and show that it is a solemn reality; for until we do this, it is useless to discuss the nature of that impotence, its seat, its extent or its cause. And it is to the inspired Word of God alone that we shall make our appeal; for if the Scriptures of truth plainly teach this doctrine, then we are on sure ground and may not reject its testimony even though no one else on earth believed it. If the divine oracles affirm it, then none of the objections brought against it by the carnal mind can have any weight with us, though in due course we shall endeavor to show that these objections are as pointless as they are groundless.

In approaching more definitely the task now before us it should be pointed out that, strictly speaking, it is the subject of human depravity which we are going to write on; yet to have so designated this section would be rather misleading as we are going to confine ourselves to only one aspect of it. The spiritual impotence of the natural man forms a distinct and separate branch of his depravity. The state of evil into which the fall has plunged us is far more dreadful and its dire consequences far more wide-reaching than is commonly supposed. The common idea is that though man has fallen he is not so badly damaged but that he may recover himself, providing he properly exercises his remaining strength or with due attention improves the help proffered him. But his case is vastly more serious than that.

A. A. Hodge said:

The three main elements involved in the consequences entailed by the sin of Adam upon his posterity are these: First, the guilt, or just penal responsibility of Adam's first sin or apostatizing act, which is imputed or judicially charged upon his descendants, whereby every child is born into the world in a state of antenatal forfeiture or condemnation. Second, the entire depravity of our nature, involving a sinful innate disposition inevitably leading to actual transgression. Third, the entire inability of the soul to change its own nature, or to do anything spiritually good in obedience to the Divine Law.

God's Word on the Subject

Let us consider some of the solemn declarations of our Lord on the third of these dire consequences of the fall. "Verily, verily, I say unto thee, Except a man be born again, he cannot see the kingdom of God" (John 3:3). Until a man is born again he remains in his natural, fallen and depraved state and so long as that is the case it is utterly impossible for him to discern or perceive divine things. Sin has both darkened his understanding and destroyed his spiritual vision. "The way of the wicked is as darkness: they know not at what they stumble" (Prov. 4:19). Though divine instruction is supplied them, though God has given them His Word in which the way to heaven is plainly marked out, still they are incapable of profiting from it. Moses represented them as groping at noonday (Deut. 28:29), and Job declares, "They meet with darkness in the daytime, and grope in the noonday as in the night" (5:14). Jeremiah depicts them as walking in "slippery ways in the darkness" (23:12).

Now this darkness which envelops the natural man is a moral one, having its seat in the soul. Our Savior declared, "The light of the body is the eye: if therefore thine eye be single, thy whole body shall be full of light. But if thine eye be evil, thy whole body shall be full of darkness. If therefore the light that is in thee be darkness, how great is that darkness!" (Matt. 6:22-23). The heart is the same to the soul as the eye is to the body. As a sound eye lets in natural light, so a good heart lets in spiritual light; and as a blind eye shuts out natural light, so an evil heart shuts out spiritual light. Accordingly we find the apostle expressly ascribing the darkness of the understanding to the blindness of the heart. He represents all men as "having the understanding darkened, being alienated from the life of God through the ignorance that is in them, because of the blindness of their heart" (Eph. 4:18).

While sinners remain under the entire dominion of a wicked heart they are altogether blind to the spiritual excellence of the character, the works and the ways of God. "Hear now this, O foolish people, and without understanding; which have eyes, and see not; which have ears, and hear not" (Jer. 5:21). The natural man is blind. This awful fact was affirmed again and again by our Lord as He addressed hypocritical scribes thus: "blind leaders of the blind," "ye blind guides," "thou blind Pharisee" (Matt. 15:14; 23:24, 26). Paul said: "The god of this world hath blinded the minds of them which believe not" (2 Cor. 4:4). There is in the unregenerate mind an incompetence, an incapacity, an inability to understand the things of the Spirit; and Christ's repeated miracle in restoring sight to the naturally blind was designed to teach us our imperative need of the same divine power recovering spiritual vision to our souls.

A question has been raised as to whether this blindness of the natural man is partial or total, whether it is simply a defect of vision or whether he has no vision at all. The nature of his disease may best be defined as spiritual myopia or shortsightedness. He is able to see clearly objects which are nearby, but distant ones lie wholly beyond the range of his vision. In other words, the mind's eye of the sinner is capable of perceiving natural things, but he has no ability to see spiritual things. Holy Writ states that the one who "lacketh these things," namely, the graces of faith, virtue, knowledge, and so forth, mentioned in 2 Peter 1:5-7, is "blind, and cannot see afar off" (v. 9). The Book therefore urges him to receive "eyesalve" from Christ, that he may see (Rev. 3:18).

For this very purpose the Son of God came into the world: to give "deliverance to the captives, and recovering of sight to the blind" (Luke 4:18). Concerning those who are the subjects of this miracle of grace it is said, "Ye were sometimes darkness, but now are ye light in the Lord" (Eph. 5:8). This is the fulfillment of our Lord's promise: "I am the light of the world: he that followeth me shall not walk in darkness, but shall have the light of life" (John 8:12). God is light, therefore those who are alienated from Him are in complete spiritual darkness. They do not see the frightful danger to which they are exposed. Though they are led captive by Satan from day to day and year to year, they are totally unaware of his malignant influence over them. They are blind to the nature and tendency of their religious performances, failing to perceive that no matter how earnestly they engage in them, they cannot be acceptable to God while their minds are at enmity against Him. They are blind to the way and means of recovery.

The awful thing is that the natural man is quite blind to the blindness of his heart which is insensibly leading him to "the blackness of darkness forever" (Jude 13). That is why the vast majority live so securely and peacefully. It has always appeared strange to the godly why the ungodly can be so unconcerned while under sentence of death, and conduct themselves so frivolously and gaily while exposed to the wrath to come. John was surprised to see the wicked spending their days in carnality and feasting. David was grieved at the prosperity of the wicked and could not account for their not being in trouble as other men. Amos was astonished to behold the sinners in Zion living at ease, putting the evil day far from them, lying on beds of ivory. Nothing but their spiritual blindness can explain the conduct of the vast majority of mankind, crying peace and safety when exposed to impending destruction.

Man's Opposition

Since all sinners are involved in such spiritual darkness as makes them unaware of their present condition and condemnation, it is not surprising that they are so displeased when their fearful danger is plainly pointed out. Such faithful warning tends to disturb their present peace and comfort and to destroy their future hopes and prospects of happiness. If they were once made to truly realize the imminent danger of the damnation of hell, their ease, security and joy would be completely dispelled. They cannot bear, therefore, to hear the plain truth respecting their wretchedness and guilt. Sinners could not bear to hear the plain teachings of the prophets or Christ on this account; this explains their bitter complaints and fierce opposition. They regard as enemies those who try to befriend them. They stop their ears and run from them.

That the natural man—even the most zealous religionist—has no perception of this spiritual blindness, and that he is highly displeased when charged with it, is evident: "Jesus said, For judgment I am come into this world, that they which see not might see; and that they which see might be made blind. And some of the Pharisees which were with him heard these words, and said unto him, Are we blind also? And Jesus said unto them, If ye were blind, ye should have no sin: but now ye say, We see; therefore your sin remaineth" (John 9:39-41). God's Son became incarnate for the purpose of bringing to light the hidden things of darkness. He came to expose things, that those made conscious of their blindness might receive sight, but that they who had spiritual sight in their own estimation should be "made blind"—judicially abandoned to the pride of their evil hearts. The infatuated Pharisees had no desire for such an experience. Denying their blindness, they were left in their sin.

"Verily, verily, I say unto thee, Except a man be born again, he cannot see the kingdom of God" (John 3:3). He cannot see the things of God because by nature he is enveloped in total spiritual darkness; even though external light shine on him, he has no eyes with which to see. "The light shineth in darkness; and the darkness comprehended it not" (John 1:5). When the Lord of life and light appeared among them, men had no eyes to see His beauty, but despised and rejected Him. And so it is still; every verse in Scripture which treats of the Spirit's illumination confirms this

solemn fact. "For God, who commanded the light to shine out of darkness, hath shined in our hearts, to give the light of the knowledge of
the glory of God in the face of Jesus Christ" (2 Cor. 4:6). This giving of
light and knowledge is by divine power, being analogous to that power
by which the light at the first creation was provided. As far as spiritual,
saving knowledge of the truth is concerned, the mind of fallen man is like
the chaos before God said "Let there be light." "Darkness was upon the
face of the deep," and in that state it is impossible for men to understand
the things of the Spirit.

Not only is the understanding of the natural man completely under the
dominion of darkness, but his will is paralyzed against good; and if that
is so, the sinner is indeed impotent. This fact was made clear by Christ
when He affirmed, "No man can come to me, except the Father which
hath sent me draw him" (John 6:44). And why is it that the sinner cannot
come to Christ by his own unaided powers? Because he has no inclination to do so and, therefore, no volition in that direction. The Greek might
be rendered "Ye will not come to me." There is not the slightest desire in
the unregenerate heart to do so.

The will of fallen man is depraved, being completely in bondage to sin.
There is not merely a negative lack of inclination, but there is a positive
disinclination. The unwillingness consists of aversion: "The carnal mind
is enmity against God: for it is not subject to the law of God, neither indeed can be" (Rom. 8:7). And not only is there an aversion against God,
there is a hatred of Him. Christ said to His disciples, "If the world hate
you, ye know that it hated me before it hated you" (John 15:18). This
hatred is inveterate obstinacy: "The Lord said unto Moses, I have seen
this people, and, behold, it is a stiffnecked people" (Exodus 32:9). "All day
long I have stretched forth my hands unto a disobedient and gainsay-
ing people" (Rom. 10:21). Man is incorrigible and in himself his case is
hopeless. "Thy people shall be willing in the day of thy power" (Ps. 110:3)
because they have no power whatever of their own to effect such willingness.

Since we have demonstrated from the Scriptures of truth that the natural man is utterly unable to discern spiritual things, much less to choose
them, there is little need for us to labor the point that he is quite incompetent to perform any spiritual act. Nor is this only a logical inference
drawn by theologians; it is expressly affirmed in the Word: "So then they
that are in the flesh cannot please God" (Rom. 8:8). There is no denying
the meaning of that terrible indictment, as there is no likelihood of its
originating with man himself. Jeremiah said, "O Lord, I know that the
way of man is not in himself: it is not in man that walketh to direct his
steps" (10:23). All power to direct our steps in the paths of righteousness
was lost by us at the fall, and therefore we are entirely dependent on God
to work in us "both to will and to do of his good pleasure" (Phil. 2:13).

Little as this solemn truth of man's moral impotence is known today
and widely as it is denied by modern thought and teaching, there was

a time when it was generally contended for. In the Thirty-nine Articles of the Church of England (to which all her ministers must still solemnly and formally subscribe) the Tenth reads thus:

The condition of man after the fall of Adam is such, that he cannot turn and prepare himself, by his own natural strength and good works to faith and calling upon God. Wherefore we have no power to do good works pleasant and acceptable to God.

In the Westminster Confession of Faith chapter 6 begins thus:

Our first parents being seduced by the subtlety and temptation of Satan, sinned in eating the forbidden fruit. This their sin God was pleased, according to His wise and holy counsel, to permit, having purposed to order it to His own glory. By this sin they fell from their original righteousness and communion with God, and so became dead in sin, and wholly defiled in all the faculties and parts of soul and body. They being the root of all mankind, the guilt of this sin was imputed, and the same death in sin and corrupted nature conveyed to all their posterity, descending from them by ordinary generation. From this original corruption, whereby we are utterly indisposed, disabled, and made opposite to all good, and wholly inclined to all evil, do proceed all actual transgressions.

Chapter 3
Nature

The doctrine we are now considering is a most solemn and forbidding one. Certainly it is one which could never have been invented by man, for it is far too humbling and distasteful. It is one which is most offensive to human pride, and at complete variance with the modem idea of the progress of the human race. Nevertheless, if we accept the Scriptures as a divine revelation, we have no choice but to uncomplainingly receive this truth. The ruined and helpless state of the sinner is fully attested by the Bible. There fallen man is represented as so utterly carnal and sold under sin as to be not only "without strength" (Rom. 5:6) but lacking the least inclination to move toward God. Very dark indeed is this side of the truth, but its supplement is the glory of God in rich grace, for it furnishes a real but necessary background to the blessed contents of the gospel.

Clear Teaching of Scripture

The Scriptures plainly teach that man is a fallen being, that he is lost (Luke 19:10), that he cannot recover himself from his ruin, that despite the fact of an all-sufficient Savior presented to him, he cannot come to Him until he is moved upon by the Spirit of God. Thus it is quite evident that if a sinner is saved, he owes his salvation entirely to the free grace and effectual power of God, and not to any good in or from or by himself. "Not unto us, O Lord, not unto us, but thy name give glory, for thy mercy" (Ps. 115:1) is the unqualified acknowledgment of all the redeemed. Scripture speaks in no uncertain language on this point. If one man differs from another on this all-important matter of being saved, then it is God who has made him to differ (1 Cor. 4:7) and not himself.

Nor is the sinner's salvation to be in any way attributed to either pliability of heart or diligence in the use of means. "So then it is not of him that willeth, nor of him that runneth, but of God that showed mercy." "Therefore hath he mercy on whom he will have mercy" (Rom. 9:16, 18). The context of John 6:44 indicates that our Lord was thus accounting for the enmity of the murmuring Jews: "No man can come to me, except the Father which hath sent me draw him." By those words Christ intimated that, considering what fallen human nature is, the conduct of His enemies is not to be wondered at; that they acted in no other way than will all other men when left to themselves; that His own disciples would never have obeyed and followed Him had not a gracious divine influence been exercised on them.

Man's Strong Objection

But as soon as this flesh-withering truth is pressed upon the unregenerate, they raise an outcry and voice their objections against it. If the
spiritual condition of fallen man is one of complete helplessness, then
how can the gospel ask him to turn from his sins and flee to Christ for
refuge? If the natural man is unable to repent and believe the gospel,
then how can he be justly punished for his impenitence and unbelief?
On what ground can man be blamed for not doing what is morally impossible? Notwithstanding these difficulties the point of doctrine which we
shall insist upon is that no one is able to comply with the terms of the
gospel until he is made the subject of the special and effectual grace of
God, that is, until he is divinely quickened, made willing, so that he actually does comply with its terms.

Nevertheless, we shall endeavor to show that sinners are not unjustly
condemned for their depravity, but that their inability is blameworthy.
Great care needs to be taken in stating this doctrine accurately. Otherwise men will be encouraged to put it to wrong use, making it a comfort-
able resting place for their corrupt hearts. By a misrepresentation of this
doctrine more than one preacher has "strengthened the hands of the
wicked, that he should not return from his wicked way" (Ezek. 13:22).
The truth of man's spiritual impotence has been so distorted that many
sinners have been made to feel that they are to be pitied, that they are
sincere in desiring a new heart— which has not yet been granted them.
Many, while excusing their helplessness, suppose this to be consistent
with a genuine longing to be renewed. It is the duty of the minister to
make his hearers realize they are under no inability except the excuseless corruption of their own hearts.

Need for Understanding the Doctrine

There is a real need for us to look closely at the precise nature of man's
spiritual inability, as to why he cannot come to Christ unless he be divinely drawn. But first let us notice some of the tenets of others on this
point. These fall into two main classes, Pelagians and Semi-Pelagians—
Pelagius being the principal opponent of the godly Augustine in the fifth
century.

A. A. Hodge in his Outlines of Theology has succinctly summarized the
Pelagian dogmas on the subject of man's ability to fulfill the law of God.
Here is the essence of his four points: (1) Moral character can be predicated only of volitions. (2) Ability is always the measure of responsibility.
(3) Hence every man has always plenary power to do all that it is his duty
to do. (4) Hence the human will alone, to the exclusion of the interfer-
ence of any internal influence from God, must decide human character
and destiny. The only divine influence needed by man or consistent with
his character as a self-determining agent is an external, providential and
educational one.

Semi-Pelagians believe thus: (1) Man's nature has been so far weakened by the fall that it cannot act right in spiritual matters without divine assistance. (2) This weakened moral state which infants inherit from their parents is the cause of sin, but not itself sin in the sense of deserving the wrath of God. (3) Man must strive to do his whole duty, when God meets him with cooperative grace and makes his efforts successful. (4) Man is not responsible for the sins he commits until after he has enjoyed and abused the influences of grace.

Arminians are Semi-Pelagians, many of them going the whole length of the error in affirming the freedom of fallen man's will toward good. But their practical contention may fairly be stated thus: Man has certainly suffered considerably from the fall, so much so that sinners are unable to do much, if anything, toward their salvation merely of themselves. Nevertheless sinners are able, by the help of common grace (supposed to be extended by the Spirit to all who hear the gospel) to do those things which are regarded as fulfilling the preliminary conditions of salvation (such as acknowledging their sins and calling on God for help to forsake them and turn to Christ). And if sinners will thus pray, use the means of grace, and put forth what power they do have, then assuredly God will meet them halfway and renew their hearts and pardon their iniquities.

We object to this belief. First, far from the Scriptures representing man as being partially disabled by the fall, they declare him to be completely ruined—not merely weakened, but "without strength" (Rom. 5:6). Second, to affirm that the natural man has any aspiration toward God is to deny that he is totally depraved, that "every imagination of the thoughts of his heart . . .[is] only evil continually" (Gen. 6:5; cf. 8:21), that "there is none that seeketh after God" (Rom. 3:11). Third, if it were true that God could not justly condemn sinners for their inability to comply with the terms of the gospel, and that in order to give every man a "fair chance" to be saved He extends to all the common help of His Spirit, that would not be "grace" but a debt which He owed to His creatures. Fourth, if such a God-insulting principle were granted, the conclusion would inevitably follow that those who improved this "common grace" could lawfully boast that they made themselves to differ from those who did not improve it.

But enough of these shifts and subterfuges of the carnal mind. Let us now turn to God's own Word and see what it teaches us concerning the nature of man's spiritual impotence. First, it represents it as being a penal one, a judicial sentence from the righteous Judge of all the earth. Unless this is clearly grasped at the outset we are left without any adequate explanation of this dark mystery. God did not create man as he now is. God made man holy and upright, and by man's own apostasy he became corrupt and wicked. The Creator originally endowed man with certain powers, placed him on probation, and prescribed a rule of conduct for him. Had our first parents preserved their integrity, had they remained in loving and loyal subjection to their Maker and Ruler, all would have been well, not only for themselves but also for their posterity. But they were not willing to remain in the place of subjection. They took the reins into their own hands, rebelling against their Governor. And the outcome was dreadful.

The sin of man was extreme and aggravated. It was committed contrary to knowledge and, through the beneficence of the One against whom it was directed, in the face of great advantages. It was committed against divine warning, and against an explicit declaration of the consequence of man's transgression. In Adam's fearful offense there were unbelief, presumption, ingratitude, rebellion against his righteous and gracious Maker. Let the dreadfulness of this first human sin be carefully weighed before we are tempted to murmur against the dire consequences which accompanied it. Those dire consequences may all be summed up in the fearful word "death," for "the wages of sin is death." The full import of that statement can best be ascertained by considering all the evil effects which have since come to man. A just, holy, sin-hating God caused the punishment to fit the crime.

Probation of Human Race in Adam

When God placed Adam on probation it pleased Him to place the whole human race on probation, for Adam's posterity were not only in him seminally as their natural head, but they were also in him legally and morally as their legal and moral head. In other words, by divine constitution and covenant Adam stood and acted as the federal representative of the whole human race. Consequently, when he sinned, we sinned; when he fell, we fell. God justly imputed Adam's transgression to all his descendants, whose agent he was: "By the offence of one judgment came upon all men to condemnation" (Rom. 5:18). By his sin Adam became not only guilty but corrupt, and that defilement of nature is transmitted to all his children. Thomas Boston said, "Adam's sin corrupted man's nature and leavened the whole lump of mankind. We putrefied in Adam as our root. The root was poisoned, and so the branches were envenomed."

"Wherefore, as by one man sin entered into the world, and death by sin; and so death passed upon all men, for that all sinned" (Rom. 5:12). We repeat that Adam was not only the father but the federal representative of his posterity. Consequently justice required that they should be dealt with as sharing in his guilt, that therefore the same punishment should be inflicted on them, which is exactly what the vitally important passage in Romans 5:12-21 affirms. "By one man [acting on behalf of the many], sin entered [as a foreign element, as a hostile factor] into the world [the whole system over which Adam had been placed as the vicegerent of God: blasting the fair face of nature, bringing a curse upon the earth, ruining all humanity], and death by sin [as its appointed wages]; and so death [as the sentence of the righteous Judge] passed upon all men [because all men were seminally and federally in Adam]."

It needs to be carefully borne in mind that in connection with the penal infliction which came upon man at the fall, he lost no moral or spiritual faculty, but rather the power to use them right. In Scripture "death" (as the wages of sin) does not signify annihilation but separation. As physical death is the separation of the soul from the body, so spiritual death is the separation of the soul from its Maker. Ephesians 4:18 expresses it as "being alienated from the life of God." Thus, when the father said of the prodigal, "This my son was dead" (Luke 15), he meant that his son had been absent from him—away in the "far country." Hence when, as the Substitute of His people, Christ was receiving in their stead the wages due them, He cried, "My God, my God, why hast thou forsaken me?" This is why the lake of fire is called "the second death"—because those cast there are "punished with everlasting destruction from the presence of the Lord" (2 Thess. 1:9).

We have said that all of Adam's posterity shared in the guilt of the great transgression committed by their federal head, and that therefore the same punishment is inflicted on them as on him. That punishment consisted (so far as its present character is concerned) in his coming under the curse and wrath of God, the corrupting of his nature, and the mortalizing of his body. Clear proof of this is found in that inspired statement "And Adam lived a hundred and thirty years, and begat a son in his own likeness, after his image" (Gen. 5:3), which is in direct antithesis to his being created "in the image of God" (Gen. 1:27). That Adam's first son was morally depraved was clearly evidenced by his conduct; and that his second son was also depraved was fully acknowledged by the sacrifice which he brought to God.

As a result of the fall man is born into this world so totally depraved in his moral nature as to be entirely unable to do anything spiritually good; furthermore, he is not in the slightest degree disposed to do good. Even under the exciting and persuasive influences of divine grace, the will of man is completely unfit to act right in cooperation with grace until the will itself is by the power of God radically and permanently renewed. The tree itself must be made good before there is the least prospect of any good fruit being borne by it. Even after a man is regenerated, the renewed will always continue dependent on divine grace to energize, direct and enable it for the performance of anything acceptable to God, as the language of Christ clearly shows: "Without me ye can do nothing" (John 15:5).

But let it be clearly understood that though man has by the fall lost all power to do anything pleasing to God, yet his Maker has not lost His authority over him nor forfeited His right to require that which is due Him. As creatures we were bound to serve God and do whatever He commanded; and the fact that we have, by our own folly and sin, thrown away the strength given to us cannot and does not cancel our obligations. Has the creditor no right to demand payment for what is owed him because the debtor has squandered his substance and is unable to pay him? If God can require of us no more than we are now able to give Him, then the more we enslave ourselves by evil habits and still further incapacitate ourselves the less our liabilities; then the deeper we plunge into sin the less wicked we would become. This is a manifest absurdity.

Even though by Adam's fall we have become depraved and spiritually helpless creatures, yet the terrible fact that we are enemies to the infinitely glorious God, our Maker, makes us infinitely to blame and without the vestige of a legitimate excuse. Surely it is perfectly obvious that nothing can make it right for a creature to voluntarily rise up at enmity against One who is the sum of all excellence, infinitely worthy of our love, homage and obedience. Thus, for man—whatever the origin of his depravity—to be a rebel against the Governor of this world is infinitely evil and culpable. It is utterly vain for us to seek shelter behind Adam's offense while every sin we commit is voluntary and not compulsory—the free, spontaneous inclination of our hearts. This being the case, every mouth will be stopped, and all the world stand guilty before God (Rom. 3:19).

To this it may be objected that the writer of Romans argued that he was not personally and properly to blame for the corruptions of his heart: "It is no more I that do it, but sin that dwelleth in me" (7:17, 20). But there is no justification for perverting the language in that passage. If the scope of the words is noted, such a misuse of them is at once ruled out. The writer was showing that divine grace and not indwelling sin was the governing principle within him—as he had affirmed previously: "Sin shall not have dominion over you: for ye are not under the law, but under grace" (6:14). Far from insinuating that he did not feel wholly blamable for his remaining corruption, he declared, "I am carnal, sold under sin" (7:14), and cried as a brokenhearted penitent, "O wretched man that I am!" (v. 24). It is perfectly obvious that he could not have mourned for his remaining corruption as being sinful if he had not felt he was to blame for them.

Man's spiritual impotence is not only penal but moral, by which we mean that he is now unable to meet the requirements of the moral law. We employ this term "moral," first of all, in contrast with "natural," for the spiritual helplessness of fallen man is unnatural, inasmuch as it does not pertain to the nature of man as created by God. Man (in Adam) was endowed with full ability to do whatever was required of him, but he lost that ability by the fall. We employ this term "moral," in the second place, because it accurately defines the character of fallen man's malady. His inability is purely moral, because while he still possesses all moral as well as intellectual faculties requisite for right action, yet the moral state of his faculties is such as to render right action impossible. A. A. Hodge said, "Its essence is in the inability of the soul to know, love, or choose spiritual good; and its ground exists in that moral corruption of soul whereby it is blind, insensible, and totally averse to all that is spiritually good."

The affirmation that fallen man is morally impotent presents a serious difficulty for many. They suppose that to assert his inability to will or do anything spiritually good is utterly incompatible with human responsibility or the sinner's guilt. These difficulties are later considered at length. But it is necessary for us to allude to these difficulties at the present stage because the effort to show the reconcilability of fallen man's inability with his responsibility has led not a few defenders of the former truth to make predications which were unwarrantable and untrue. They have felt that there is, there must be, some sense or respect in which even fallen man may be said to be able to will and do what is required of him; and they have labored to show in what sense this ability exists, while at the same time man is, in another sense, unable.

Many Calvinists have supposed that in order to avoid the awful error of Antinomian fatalism it was necessary to ascribe some kind of ability to fallen man, and therefore they have resorted to the distinction between natural and moral inability. They have affirmed that though man is now morally unable to do what God requires, yet he has a natural ability to do it, and therefore is responsible for not doing it. In the past we ourselves have made use of this distinction, and we still believe it to be a real and important one, though we are now satisfied that it is expressed faultily. There is a radical difference between a person being in possession of natural or moral faculties, and his possessing or not possessing the power to use those faculties right. And in the accurate stating of these considerations lies the difference between the preservation of the doctrine of man's depravity and moral impotence, and the repudiation or at least the whittling down of it.

At this very point many have burdened their writings with a metaphysical discussion of the human will, a discussion so abstruse that comparatively few of their readers possessed the necessary education or mentality to intelligently follow it. We do not propose to discuss such questions as Is the will of fallen man free? If so, in what sense? To introduce such an inquiry here would divert attention too much from the more important query, Can man by any efforts of his own recover himself from the effects of the fall? Suffice it, then, to insist that the sinner's unwillingness to come to Christ is far more than a mere negation or a not putting forth of such a volition. It is a positive thing, an active aversion to Him, a terrible and inveterate enmity against Him.

Impossibility of Moral Obedience

The term "ability," or "power," is not easy to define, for it is a relative term, having reference to something to be done or resisted. Thus when we meet with the word, the mind at once asks, Power to do what? Ability to resist what? The particular kind of ability necessary is determined by the particular kind of action to be performed. If it is the lifting of a heavy weight, physical ability is needed; if the working out of a sum in arithmetic, mental power; if the choosing between good and evil, moral power. Man has sufficient physical and intellectual ability to keep many of the precepts of the moral law, yet no possible expenditure of such power could produce moral obedience. It may be that Gabriel has less natural and intellectual power than Satan. Suppose it is so, then what? The conclusion is simply that no amount of ability can go beyond its own kind.

Love to God can never proceed from the powers possessed by Satan.

Let us now consider what the Scriptures teach concerning the bodily, mental and moral abilities of fallen man. First, they teach that his bodily faculties are in a ruined state, that his physical powers are enfeebled, and this as a result of sin. "By one man sin entered into the world, and death by sin" (Rom. 5:12). None of our readers is likely to deny that this includes physical death. Now death necessarily implies a failure of the powers of the body. Sickness, feebleness, the wasting of the physical energies and tissues are included. And all of these originate in sin as their moral cause, and are the penal results of it. Every aching joint, every quivering nerve, every pang of pain we experience, is a reminder and mark of God's displeasure on the original misuse of our bodily powers in the garden of Eden.

Second, man's intellectual powers have suffered by the fall. "Having the understanding darkened, being alienated from the life of God through the ignorance that is in them, because of the blindness of their heart" (Eph. 4:18). A very definite display of this ignorance was made by our first parents after their apostasy. Their sin consisted in allowing their affections to wander after a forbidden object, seeking their happiness not in the delightful communion of God but in the suggestion presented to them by the tempter. Like their descendants ever since, they loved and served the creature more than the Creator. Their conduct in hiding from God showed an alienation of affections. Had their delight been in the Lord as their chief good, then desire for concealment could not have possessed their minds. That foolish attempt to hide themselves from the searching eye of God betrayed their ignorance as well as their conscious guilt. Had not their foolish hearts been darkened, such an attempt would not have been made. "Professing themselves to be wise, they became fools" (Rom. 1:22).

This mental darkness, this ignorance of mind, is insuperable to man unaided by supernatural grace. Fallen man never would, never could, dispel this darkness, overcome this ignorance. He labors under mental paucity to such a degree as to make it impossible for him to attain to the true knowledge of God and to understand the things of the Spirit. He has an understanding by which he may know natural things: he can reason, investigate truth, and learn much of God's wisdom as it is displayed in the works of creation. He is capable of knowing the moral truths of God's Word as mere abstract propositions; but a true, spiritual, saving apprehension of them is utterly beyond his unaided powers. There is a positive defect and inability in his mind. "The natural man receiveth not the things of the Spirit of God: for they are foolishness unto him: neither can he know them, because they are spiritually discerned" (1 Cor. 2:14).

The Natural Man

By the "natural man" is unquestionably meant the unrenewed man, the man in whom the miracle of regeneration and illumination has not been effected. The context makes this clear: "Now we [Christians] have received, not the spirit of the world, but the Spirit which is of God" (v. 12). And for what end had the Spirit been given to them? That they might be delivered from their chains of ignorance, that their inability of mind might be removed so that they "might know the things that are freely given to us of God." "Which things [of the Spirit] also we speak, not in the words which man's wisdom teacheth, but which the Holy Ghost teacheth; comparing spiritual things with spiritual" (v. 13). Here is a contrast between man's wisdom and its teachings, and the Spirit's wisdom and His teachings. That the natural man" of verse 14 is unregenerate is further seen from contrasting him with the "spiritual" man in verse 15.

A divine explanation is here given as to why the natural man does not receive the things of the Spirit of God. It is a most cogent and solemn one: "For they are foolishness unto him." That is, he rejects them because they are absurd to his apprehension. It is contrary to the very nature of the human mind to receive as truth that which it thinks is preposterous. And why do the things of the Spirit of God appear as foolishness to the natural man? Are they not in themselves the consummation of wisdom? Wisdom is not folly; no, yet it may appear as such and be so treated, even by minds which in other matters are of quick and accurate perception. The wisdom of the higher mathematician is foolishness to the illiterate. Why? Because he cannot understand it; he does not have the power of mind to comprehend the mighty thoughts of a Newton.

Why are the things of the Spirit of God beyond the comprehension of the natural man? Do not many of the unregenerate possess vigorous and clear-thinking minds? Can they not reason accurately when they have perceived clearly? Have not some of the unconverted given the most illustrious displays of the powers of the human intellect? Why, then, cannot they know the things of the Spirit? This too is answered by 1 Corinthians 2:14. Those things require a peculiar power of discernment, which the unrenewed have not: "They are spiritually discerned." And the natural man is not spiritual. Until the natural man is taught of God—until the eyes of his understanding are enlightened (Eph. 1:18)—he will never see any beauty in the Christ of God or any wisdom in the Spirit of God.

If further proof of the mental inability of the natural man is needed, it is furnished in those passages which speak of the Spirit's illumination. "God, who commanded the light to shine out of darkness, hath shined in our hearts, to give the light of the knowledge of the glory of God in the face of Jesus Christ" (2 Cor. 4:6). Hence, "the spirit of wisdom and revelation in the knowledge of him" is said to be the gift of the Father (Eph. 1:17). Previous to that gift, "ye were sometimes darkness, but now are ye light in the Lord" (Eph. 5:8). "But the anointing which ye have received of him abideth in you, and ye need not that any man teach you" (1 John 2:27). From these passages it is evident (1) that the mind of man is in a state of spiritual darkness; (2) that it continues, and will continue so, until the Spirit of God gives it light or knowledge; (3) that this giving of light or knowledge is by divine power, a miracle of grace, as truly a miracle as when at the beginning the Lord said, "Let there be light."

Some have objected that man possesses the organ of vision, and therefore he has the ability to see, although he does not have the light. Simply remove the obstructing shutters and the prisoner in his dungeon will see. But let us not be deceived by such sophistry. It is not true that man having a sound eye has the ability to see. It is often contrary to facts, both naturally and spiritually. Without light he cannot see, he has not the ability to do so. Indeed, those with sound eyes and light cannot see all things, even things which are perceptible to others; myopia, or nearsightedness, hinders. A man who may be able to see with the mind's eye a simple proposition cannot see the force of a profound argument.

Third, the moral powers of man's soul are paralyzed by the fall. Darkness on the understanding, ignorance in the mind, corruption of the affections, must of necessity radically affect motives and choice. To insist that either the mind or the will has a power to act contrary to motive is a manifest absurdity, for in that case it would not be a moral act at all. The very essence of morality is a capacity to be influenced by considerations of right and wrong. Were a rational mind to act without any motive—a contradiction in terms—it certainly would not be a moral act. Motives are simply the mind's view of things, influencing to action; and since the understanding has been blinded by sin and the affections so corrupted, it is obvious that until man is renewed he will reject the good and choose the evil.

Man's Bias Toward Evil

As we have already pointed out, man is unwilling to choose the good because he is disinclined to it, and he chooses evil because his heart is biased toward it. Men love darkness rather than light. Surely no proof of such assertions is needed; all history too sadly testifies to their verity. It is a waste of breath to ask for evidence that man is inclined to evil as the sparks fly upward. Common observation and our own personal consciousness alike bear witness to this lamentable fact. It is equally plain that it is the derangement of the mind by sin which affects the moral power of perceiving right and wrong enfeebling or destroying the force of moral motives.

An unregenerate and a regenerate man may contemplate the same subject matter, view the same objects; but how different their moral perceptions! Therefore their motives and actions will be quite different. The things seen by their minds being different, diverse effects are necessarily produced on them. The one sees a "root out of a dry ground" in which there is "no form nor comeliness," whereas the other sees One who is "altogether lovely." In consequence, our Lord is despised and rejected by the former, whereas He is loved and embraced by the latter. While such are the views (perceptions) of the two individuals, respectively, such must be their choice and conduct. It is impossible to be otherwise. Their moral perception must be changed before it is possible for their volitions to be altered.

Such is the ruined condition of the fallen creature. No human power is able to effect any alteration in the moral perceptions of sinful men. "Can the Ethiopian change his skin, or the leopard his spots? Then may ye also do good, that are accustomed to do evil" (Jer. 13:23). Nothing short of the sinner, mentally and morally blind to divine light. Here, then, lies the moral inability of the natural man: it consists in the lack of adequate powers of moral perception. His moral sense is prostrated, his mind unable to properly discern between good and evil, truth and falsehood, God and Mammon, Christ and Belial. Not that he can perceive no difference, but that he cannot appreciate in any tolerable degree the excellence of truth or the glory of its Author. He cannot discern the real baseness of falsehood or the degradation of vice.

It is a great mistake to suppose that fallen man possesses adequate faculties for such moral perception, and lacks only the necessary moral light. The very opposite is the actual case. Moral light shines all around him, but his powers of vision are gone. He walks in darkness while the midday splendors of the sun of righteousness shine all around him. Fables are regarded as truth, but the truth itself is rejected. Shadows are chased, but the substance is ignored. The gospel is "hid to them that are lost" (2 Cor. 4:3). When the Lord is presented to sinners, they "see in him no beauty that they should desire him." So blind is the natural man that he gropes in the noonday and stumbles over the rock of ages. And unless a sovereign God is pleased to have mercy on him, his moral blindness continues until he passes out into the "blackness of darkness forever."

The deprivation of our nature consists not in the absence of intelligence, but in the ability to use our reason in a wise and fit manner. That which man lost at the fall was not a faculty but a principle. He still retains everything which is requisite to constitute him a rational, moral and responsible being; but he threw away that uprightness which secured the approbation of God. He lost the principle of holiness and, with it, all power to keep the moral law. Nor is this all; a foreign element—an element diametrically opposed to God—entered into man, corrupting his whole being. The principle of holiness was supplanted by the principle of sin, and this has rendered man utterly unable to act in a spiritual manner. True, he may mechanically or imitatively perform spiritual acts (such as praying), yet he cannot perform them in a spiritual manner— from spiritual motives and for spiritual ends. He has no moral ability to do so. True, he can do many things, but none rightly—in a way pleasing to God.

Spiritual good is holiness, and holiness consists in supreme love of God and equal love of men. Fallen man, alone and of himself, is utterly unable to love God with all his soul and strength, and his neighbor as himself. This principle of holy love is completely absent from his heart, nor can he by any effort beget such an affection within himself. He is utterly unable to originate within his will any inclination or disposition that is spiritually good; he has not the moral power to do so. Moral power is nothing more nor less than a holy nature with holy dispositions; it is the perception of the beauty of God and the response of the heart to the excellence and glory of God, with the consequent subjection of the will to His royal law of liberty. J. Thornwell said, "Spiritual perceptions, spiritual delight, spiritual choice, these and these alone, constitute ability to good."

In our efforts to carefully define and describe the precise character of fallen man's inability to do anything which is pleasing to God, we have shown, first, that the impotence under which he now labors is a penal one, judicially inflicted upon him by the righteous Judge of all the earth, because of his misuse of the faculties with which he was originally endowed in Adam. Second, we noted that his spiritual helplessness is a moral one, having its seat in the soul or moral nature. The principle of holiness was lost by man when he apostatized from his Maker and Governor, and the principle of sin entered his soul, corrupting the whole of his being, so that he is no longer capable of rendering any spiritual obedience to the moral law; that is, he is incapable of obeying it from spiritual motives and with spiritual designs.

We pass on now to show, third, that fallen man's inability is voluntary. Some of our readers who have had no difficulty in following us through the first two sections are likely to demur here. We refer to hyper-Calvinists who have such a one-sided conception of man's spiritual helplessness that they have lapsed into serious error. They look upon the condition and case of the sinner much as they do those people who have suffered a stroke which has paralyzed their limbs: as a calamity and not the result of a crime, as something which necessitates a state of inertia and inactivity, as something which annuls their responsibility. They fail to see that the moral impotence of the natural man is deliberate and therefore highly culpable.

Before appealing to the Scriptures for proofs of this third point, we must explain the sense in which we use our term. In affirming that the moral and sinful inability of fallen man is a voluntary one, we mean that he acts freely and spontaneously, unforced either from within or without. This is an essential element of an accountable being, everywhere recognized and acknowledged among men. Human law (much less divine) does not hold a person to be guilty if he has been compelled by others to do wrong against his own will and protests. In all moral action the human will is self-inclined, acting freely according to the dictates of the mind, which are in turn regulated by the inclination of the heart. Though the mind be darkened and the heart corrupted, nevertheless the will acts freely and the individual remains a voluntary agent.

Some of the best theologians have drawn a distinction between the liberty and ability of the sinner's will, affirming the former but denying the latter. We believe this distinction to be accurate and helpful. Unless a person is free to exercise volitions as he pleases, he cannot be an accountable being. Nevertheless, fallen man cannot, by any exercise of will, change his nature or make any choice contrary to the governing tendencies of indwelling sin. He totally lacks any disposition to meet the requirements of the moral law, and therefore he cannot make himself willing to do so. The affections of the heart and the perceptions of the mind regulate our volitions, and the will has no inherent power to change our affections; we cannot by any resolution, however strong or prolonged, make ourselves love what we hate or hate what we love.

Because the sinner acts without any external compulsion, according to his own inclinations, his mind is free to consider and weigh the various motives which come before it, making its own preferences or choices. By motives we mean those reasons or inducements which are presented to the mind tending to lead to choice and action. The power or force of these inducements lies not in themselves (abstractedly considered), but in the state of the person who is the subject of them; consequently that which would be a powerful motive in the view of one mind would have no weight at all in the view of another. For example, the offer of a bribe would be a sufficient motive to induce one judge to decide a case contrary to law and against the evidence; whereas to another such an offer, far from being a motive to such an evil course, would be highly repulsive.

Let this be clearly grasped by the reader: Those external inducements which are presented to the mind affect a person according to the state of his or her heart. The temptation presented by Potiphar's wife, which was firmly refused by Joseph, would have been a motive of sufficient power to ruin many a youth of less purity of heart. External motives can have no influence over the choice and conduct of men except as they make an appeal to desires already existing in the mind. Throw a lighted match into a barrel of gunpowder and there is at once an explosion; but throw that match into a barrel of water and no harm is done. "The prince of this world cometh, and hath nothing in me" (John 14:30) said the holy One of God. None among the children of men can make such a claim.

Freedom of Human Will

All the affections of the human heart are, in their very nature, free. The idea of compelling a man to love or hate any object is manifestly absurd. The same holds good of all his faculties. Conscience may be enlightened and made more sensitive, or it may be resisted and hardened; but no man can be compelled to act contrary to its dictates without depriving him of his freedom, and at the same time of his responsibility. So of his will or volition: two or more alternatives confront a man, conflicting motives are presented to his mind, and his will is quite free in making a preference or choice between them. Nevertheless, it is the very nature of his will to choose that which is preferable, that which is most agreeable to his heart. Consequently, though the will acts freely, it is biased by the corruptions of the heart and therefore is unable to choose spiritual good. The heart must be changed before the will chooses God.

Against our assertion that the spiritual impotence of fallen man is a voluntary one, it may be objected that the sinner is so strongly tempted, so powerfully influenced by Satan and so thoroughly under his control that (in many instances, at least) he cannot help himself, being irresistibly drawn into sinning. That there is some force in this objection is readily granted, but we can by no means allow the length to which it is carried. However subtle the craft, however influential the sophistry, however great the power of the devil, these must not be used to repudiate our personal responsibility and criminality in sinning, nor must we construe ourselves into being his innocent dupes or unwilling victims. Never does Scripture so represent the matter; rather, we are told "Resist the devil, and he will flee from you" (Jam. 4:7). And if we seek grace to meet the conditions (specified in 1 Pet. 5:8-9), God will assuredly make good His promise.

Satan's power is not physical but moral. He has intimate access to the faculties of our souls, and though he cannot (like the Holy Spirit) work at their roots so as to change and transform their tendencies, he can ply them with representations and delusions which effectually incline them to will and do according to his good pleasure. He can cheat the understanding with appearances of truth, fascinate the fancy with pictures of beauty, and mock the heart with semblances of good. By a secret suggestion he can give an impulse to our thoughts and turn them into channels which serve the purposes of his malignity. But in all of this he does no violence to the laws of our nature. He disturbs neither the spontaneity of the understanding nor the freedom of the will. He cannot make us do a thing without our own consent, thus in consenting to his evil suggestions lies our guilt.

That sinners act freely and voluntarily in all their wrongdoing is taught throughout the Scriptures. Take, first of all, the horrible state of the heathen, a dark picture of whom is painted for us in Romans 1. There we see the consummation of human depravity. Heathenism is the full development of the principle of sin in its workings upon the intellectual, moral and religious nature of man. In Romans 1 we are shown that the dreadful condition in which the heathen now lie (and missionaries bear clear witness that what comes before their notice accurately corresponds to what is here stated) is the consequence of their own voluntary choice. "When they knew God, they glorified him not as God" (v. 21). They "changed the glory of the uncorruptible God into an image made like to corruptible man" (v. 23). They "changed the truth of God into a lie" (v. 25). They "did not like to retain God in their knowledge" (v. 28).

Nor was it any different with the favored people of Israel. So averse were they to God and His ways that they hated, persecuted and killed those messengers whom He sent to reclaim them from their wickedness. "They kept not the covenant of God, and refused to walk in his law" (Ps. 78:10). They said, "I have loved strangers, and after them will 1 go" (Jer. 2:25). "Thus saith the Lord, Stand ye in the ways, and see, and ask for the old paths, where is the good way, and walk therein, and ye shall find rest for your souls. But they said, We will not walk therein. Also I set watchmen over you saying, Hearken to the sound of the trumpet. But they said, We will not hearken" (Jer. 6:16-17). The Lord called to them, but they "refused." He stretched forth His hand, but "no man regarded." They set at nought all His counsel, and would heed none of His reproofs (Prov. 1:24-25). "The Lord God of their fathers sent to them by his messengers, rising up betimes, and sending.

But they mocked the messengers of God, and despised his words, and misused his prophets, until the wrath of the Lord rose against his people, till there was no remedy" (2 Chron. 36:15-16). God's blessed Son did not receive any better treatment at their hands. Though He appeared before them in "the form of a servant," He did not appeal to their proud hearts. Though He was "full of grace and truth," they despised and rejected Him. Though He sought only their good, they returned Him nought but evil. Though He proclaimed glad tidings for them, they refused to listen. Though He worked the most wonderful miracles before them, yet they would not believe Him. "He came unto his own, and his own received him not" (John 1:11). Their retort was "We will not have this man to reign over us" (Luke 19:14). It was a voluntary and deliberate refusal of Him. It is this very voluntariness of their sin which shall be charged against them in the day of judgment, for then shall He give order thus: "But those mine enemies, which would not that I should reign over them, bring hither, and slay them before me" (Luke 19:27).

And from whence did such wicked treatment of the Son of God proceed? From the vile corruptions of their own hearts. "They hated me without a cause" (John 15:25) declared the incarnate Son of God. There was absolutely nothing whatever either in His character or conduct which merited their wicked contempt and enmity. Did anyone force them to be of such an abominable disposition? Surely not; they were hearty in it. Were they of such bad temper against their wills? No indeed. They were voluntary in their wicked hatred of Christ. They loved darkness. They were infatuated by their corruptions and delighted in gratifying them. They were highly pleased with false prophets, because they preached in their favor, flattering them and gratifying their evil hearts. But they hated whatever was disagreeable to their evil ways.

Mistreatment of Christ's Followers

It was the same with those who heard the ambassadors of Christ, except for those in whom the sovereign God wrought a miracle of grace. Jews and Gentiles alike willfully opposed and rejected the gospel. In some cases their hatred of the truth was less openly manifested than in others; nevertheless, it was just as real. And the disrelish of and opposition to the gospel was entirely voluntary on the part of its enemies. Did not the Jewish leaders act freely when they threw Peter and John into prison? Did not the murderers of Stephen act freely when they "stopped their ears, and ran upon him with one accord" (Acts 7:57)? Did not the Philippians act freely when they "rose up together" against Paul and Silas, beat them, and cast them into prison?

The same thing obtains everywhere today. If the gospel of Christ is preached in its purity and all its glory, it does not gain the regard of the masses who hear it. Instead, as soon as the sermon is over, like the generality of the Jews in our Lord's day, they make light of it and go their ways, "one to his farm, another to his merchandise" (Matt. 22:5). They are too indifferent to seek after obtaining even a doctrinal knowledge of the truth. There are many who regard this dullness of the unsaved as mere indifference, but it is actually something far worse: it is dislike of the heart for God, deliberate opposition to Him. "They are like the deaf adder that stoppeth her ear; which will not hearken to the voice of charmers, charming never so wisely" (Ps. 58:4-5). As Paul declared in his day, "The heart of this people is waxed gross, and their ears are dull of hearing, and their eyes have they closed; lest they should see with their eyes, and hear with their ears, and understand with their heart, and should be converted" (Acts 28:27).

"They say unto God, Depart from us; for we desire not the knowledge of thy ways" (Job 21:14). Such is the desperately wicked state of man's heart, diametrically opposite to the divine excellences. Yet when this solemn truth is pressed on the unregenerate, many of them will strongly object, denying that there is any such contrariety in their hearts, saying, "I have never hated God, but have always loved Him." Thus they flatter themselves and seek to make themselves out to be far different from what they are. Nor are they wittingly lying when they make such a claim; rather, they are utterly misled by their deceitful hearts. The scribes and Pharisees truly thought that they loved God and that, had they lived in the days of their forefathers, they would not have put the prophets to death (Matt. 23:29-30). They were altogether insensible to their fearful and inveterate enmity against God; nevertheless it was there, and it later unmistakably displayed itself when they hounded the Son of God to death.

Why was it that the scribes and Pharisees were quite unconscious of the opposition of their hearts to the divine nature? It was because they had erroneous notions of the divine Being and loved only that false image which they had framed in their own imaginations; therefore they had false conceptions of the prophets which their fathers hated and murdered, and hence supposed they would have loved them. But when God was manifested in Christ, they hated Him with bitter hatred. In like manner there are multitudes of sinners today, millions in Christendom who persuade themselves that they truly love God, when in reality they hate Him; and the hardest of all tasks confronting the ministers of Christ is to shatter this cherished delusion and bring their unsaved hearers face to face with the horrible reality of their unspeakably vile condition.

Loudly as our deluded fellow creatures may boast of their love of the divine nature, as soon as they pass out of time into eternity and discover what God is, their spurious love immediately vanishes and their enmity bursts forth in full force. Sinners today do not perceive their contrariety to the divine nature because they are utterly ignorant of the true God. It must be so, for a sinful nature and a holy nature are diametrically opposite. Christendom has invented a false "God," a "God" without any sovereign choice, a "God" who loves all mankind, a "God" whose justice is swallowed up in His mercy. Were they acquainted with the God of Holy Writ—who "hatest all workers of iniquity" (Ps. 5:5), who will one day appear "in flaming fire taking vengeance on them that know not God, and that obey not the gospel of our Lord Jesus Christ: who shall be punished with everlasting destruction from the presence of the Lord" (2 Thess. 1:8-9)—they, if they honestly examined their hearts, would be conscious of the hatred they bear Him.

Guilt of Natural Man

The spiritual inability of the natural man is a criminal one. This follows inevitably from the fact that his impotence is a moral and voluntary one. It is highly important that we should be brought to see, feel and own that our spiritual helplessness is culpable, for until we do so we shall never truly justify God nor condemn ourselves. To realize oneself to be equally "without strength" and "without excuse" is deeply humiliating, and fallen man will strive with all his might to stifle such a conviction and deny the truth of it. Yet until we place the blame of our sinfulness where it really belongs, we shall not, we cannot, either vindicate the righteousness of the divine law or appreciate the marvelous grace made known in the gospel. To condemn ourselves as God condemns us is the one prerequisite to establish our title to salvation in Christ.

John Newton wrote:

We cannot ascribe too much to the grace of God; but we should be careful that, under a semblance of exalting His grace, we do not furnish the slothful and unfaithful (Matt. 25: 16) with excuses for their willfulness and wickedness. God is gracious; but let man be justly responsible for his own evil and not presume to state his case so as would, by just consequence, represent the holy God as being the cause of the sin which He hates and forbids.

That was indeed a timely word. Unfortunately, some who claim to be great admirers of Newton's works have sadly failed to uphold the responsibility of the sinner, and have so expressed his spiritual inability as to furnish him with much excuse for his sloth and infidelity. Only by insisting on the criminality of fallen man's impotence can such a deplorable snare be avoided. Inexorably as man's criminality attaches to his free agency in the committing of sin, yet the sinner will strive with might and main to avoid such a conclusion and seek to throw the blame on someone else. He will haughtily ask, "Would any right-minded person blame a man whose arms had been broken because he could no longer perform manual labor, or condemn a blind man because he did not read? Then why should I be held guilty for not performing spiritual duties which are altogether beyond my powers?"

To this difficulty several replies may be made: (1) There is no analogy in the cases advanced. Broken arms and sightless eyes are incompetent members; but the intellectual and moral faculties have not been destroyed, and it is because of misuse of these that the sinner is justly held culpable. (2) Not only does he fail to use his moral faculties in the performing of spiritual good, but he employs them in the doing of moral evil; and the excuse that he cannot help himself is an idle one.

Apply that principle to the commercial transactions of society, and what would be the result? A man contracts a debt within the compass of his present financial ability to meet. He then perversely and wickedly squanders his money and gambles away his property, so that he is no longer able to pay what he owes. Is he therefore not bound to pay? Has his reckless prodigality freed him from all moral obligation to discharge his debts? Must justice break her scales and no more hold an equal balance because he chooses to be a villain? No indeed; unregenerate men would not allow such reasoning.

To this it may be objected, "I did not bring this depravity upon myself, but was born with it. If my heart is altogether evil and I did not make it so, if such a heart was given me without my choice and consent, then how can I be to blame for its inevitable issues and actions?" Such a question betrays the fact that a wicked heart is regarded as a calamity which man did not choose, but which must be endured. It is contemplated as a thing not at all faulty in its own nature; if there is any blame attaching to it, it must be for something previous to it and of quite another kind. A person born diseased is not personally to blame, but if the disease is the result of his own indiscretion it is a just retribution. But to reason thus about sin is utterly erroneous, as if it were no sin to be a sinner or to commit sin when one has an inclination to do so, but to bring a sinful predisposition upon oneself would be a wicked thing.

Stripped of all disguise and ambiguity, the above objection amounts to this: Adam was in reality the only sinner; and we, his miserable offspring, being by nature depraved, are under a necessity of sinning, therefore cannot be to blame for it. The fact that sin itself is sinful is lost sight of. Scripture traces all our evil acts back to a sinful heart, and teaches that this is a blamable thing in itself. A depraved heart is a moral thing, being something quite different from a weak head, a bad memory or a frail constitution. A man is not to blame for these infirmities, providing he has not brought them upon himself. To say that I cannot help hating God and opposing my neighbor, and that therefore I am not to blame for doing so, certainly makes me out to be a vile and insensible scoundrel.

In order for a fallen creature to be blameworthy for his evil tendencies, it is not necessary that he should first be virtuous or free from moral corruption. If a person now finds that he is a sinner, and that from the heart he approves and chooses rebellion against God and His law, he is not the less a sinner because he has been of the same disposition for many years and has always sinned from his birth. His having sinned from the beginning, and having done nothing else, cannot be a legitimate excuse for sinning now. Nor is man's guilt the less because sin is so deeply and so thoroughly fixed in his heart. The stronger the enmity against God, the greater its heinousness. Disinclination Godward is the very essence of depravity. When we rightly define the nature of man's inability to do good—namely, a moral and a voluntary inability (not the absence of faculties, but the misuse of them) —then this excuse of blamelessness is at once exposed.

But the carnal mind will still object. We are natively no other way than God has made us; therefore if we are born sinful and God has created us thus, then He, not ourselves, is the Author of sin. To such awful lengths is the enmity of the carnal mind capable of going: shifting the onus from his own guilty shoulders and throwing the blame upon the thrice holy God. But this objection was earlier obviated. God made man upright, but he apostatized. Man ruined himself. God endowed each of us with rationality, with a conscience, with a will to refuse the evil and choose the good. It is by the free exercise of our faculties that we sin, and we have no more justification for transferring the guilt from ourselves to someone else than Adam had to blame Eve or Eve the serpent.

But is it consistent with the divine perfections to bring mankind into the world under such handicapped and wretched circumstances? "Nay but, O man, who art thou that repliest against God? Shall the thing formed say to him that formed it, Why hast thou made me thus?" (Rom. 9:20). It is blasphemous to say that it is not consistent with the divine perfections for God to do what in fact He does. It is a matter of fact that we are born into the world destitute of the moral image of God, ignorant of Him, insensible of His infinite glory. It is a plain matter of fact that in consequence of this deprivation we are disposed to love ourselves supremely, live to ourselves ultimately, and wholly delight in what is not of God. And it is clearly evident that this tendency is in direct contrariety to God's holy law and is exceedingly sinful. Whether or not we can see the justice and wisdom of this divine providence, we must remember that God is "holy in all his ways, and righteous in all his works."

But how can the sinner possibly be to blame for his evil inclination when it was Adam who corrupted human nature? The sinner is an enemy to the infinitely glorious God, and that voluntarily; therefore he is infinitely to blame and without excuse, for nothing can make it right for a creature to be deliberately hostile to his Creator. Nothing can possibly extenuate such a crime. Such hostility is in its own nature infinitely wrong, and therefore the sinner stands guilty before God. The very fact that in the day of judgment every mouth will be stopped (Rom. 3:19) shows there is no validity or force to this objection. It is for the acting out of his nature-instead of its mortifying—that the sinner is held accountable. The fact that we are born traitors to God cannot cancel our obligation to give Him allegiance. No man can escape from the righteous requirements of law by a voluntary opposition to it.

The fact that man's sinful nature is the direct consequence of Adam's transgression does not in the slightest degree make it any less his own sin or render him any less blameworthy. This is clear not only from the justice of the principle of representation (Adam's acting as our federal head), but also from the fact that each of us approves of Adam's transgression by emulating his example, joining ourselves with him in rebellion against God. That we go on to break the covenant of works and disobey the divine law demonstrates that we are righteously condemned with Adam. Because each descendant of Adam voluntarily prolongs and perpetuates in himself the evil inclination originated by his first parents, he is doubly guilty. If not, why do we not repudiate Adam and refuse to sin—stand out in opposition to him, and be holy? If we resent our being corrupted through Adam, why not break the involvement of sin?

But let us turn from these objections to the positive side of our subject. The Scriptures uniformly teach that fallen man's moral and voluntary inability is a criminal one, that God justly holds him guilty both for his depraved state and for all his sinful actions. So plain is this, so abundantly evidenced, that there is little need for us to labor the point. The first three chapters of Romans are expressly devoted to this solemn theme. There it is declared, "The wrath of God is revealed from heaven against all ungodliness and unrighteousness of men, who hold the truth in unrighteousness" (1:18). The reason for this is given in verses 19-20, ending with the inexorable sentence "They are without excuse." Chapter 2 opens with "Therefore thou art inexcusable, O man," and in 3:19 the apostle shows that the ruling of the divine law is such that, in the day to come, "every mouth may be stopped, and all the world may become guilty before God."

The criminality of the sinner's depravity and moral impotence is clearly brought out in Matthew 25:14-30. The general design of that parable is easily perceived. The "lord" of the servants signifies the Creator as the Owner and Governor of this world. The "servants" represent mankind in general. The different "talents" depict the faculties and powers with which God has endowed us, the privileges and advantages by which He distinguishes one person from another. The two servants who faithfully improved their talents picture the righteous who serve God with fidelity. The slothful and unfaithful servant portrays the sinner, who entirely neglects the service of God and blames Him rather than himself for his negligence. His grievance in verses 24-25 expresses the feelings of every impenitent sinner, who complains that God requires from him (holiness) what He has not given to him (a holy heart). This servant's condemnation was on the ground that he did not improve what he did have (v. 27)—his rational faculties and moral powers. "Cast ye the unprofitable servant into outer darkness" (v. 30) shows the justice of his condemnation.

Excuses of Natural Man

The excuse that we cannot help being so perverse is further ruled out of court by Christ's declarations to the scribes and Pharisees. They had no heart either for Christ or His doctrine. He told them plainly, "Why do ye not understand my speech? Even because ye cannot hear my word" (John 8:43). But their inability was no excuse for them in His accounting, for He affirmed that all their impotence rose from their evil hearts, their lack of a holy makeup: "Ye are of your father the devil, and the lusts of your father ye will [desire to] do" (v. 44). Though they had no more power to help themselves than we have, and were no more able to transform their hearts than we are, nevertheless our Lord judged them to be wholly to blame and altogether inexcusable, saying of them, "If I had not come and spoken unto them, they had not had sin: but now they have . . . [no excuse] for their sin (John 15:22).

Let it be specifically pointed out that when Scripture affirms the inability of a man to do good, it never does so by way of excuse. Thus, when Jehovah asked Israel, "Can the Ethiopian change his skin, or the leopard his spots? Then may ye also do good, that are accustomed to do evil" (Jer. 13:23), it was not for the purpose of mitigating their guilt, but with the object of showing how it aggravated their obstinacy of heart and to evince that no external means could affect their recovery. Just as likely was an Ethiopian to be moved by exhortation to change the color of his skin as were rebels against God to be moved by appeals to renounce their iniquities.

"Because I tell you the truth, ye believe me not. Which of you convinceth me of sin? And if I say the truth, why do ye not believe me? He that is of God heareth God's words: ye therefore hear them not, because ye are not of God" (John 8:45-47). Those cutting interrogations of our Lord proceeded on the supposition that His listeners could have received the teaching of Christ if it had been agreeable to their corrupt nature; it being otherwise, they could not understand or receive it. In like manner, when He affirmed, "No man can come to me, except the Father which hath sent me draw him," Christ did not intimate that any natural man honestly desired to come to Him, but was deterred from doing so against his will; rather, He meant that man is incapable of freely doing that which is inconsistent with his corruptions. They were averse to come to the holy Redeemer because they were in love with sin.

The excuse that I cannot help doing wrong is worthless. To plead my inability to do good simply because I lack the heart to do it would be laughed out of court even among men. Does anyone suppose that only the lack of a will to earn his living excuses a man from doing so, just as bodily infirmity does? Does anyone imagine that the covetous miser, who has no heart to give a penny to the poor, is for that reason excused from deeds of charity as one who has nothing to give? A man's heart being fully set to do evil does not render his wicked actions the less evil. If it did, it would necessarily follow that the worse any sinner grows, the less he is to blame. Nothing could be more absurd.

Let us show yet further the utter worthlessness of those evasions by which the sinner seeks to deny the criminality of his moral impotence. Men never resort to such silly reasonings when they are wronged by others. When treated with disrespect and animosity by their associates, they never offer the excuses for them behind which they seek to hide their own sins. If someone deliberately robbed me, would I say, "Poor fellow, he could not help himself; Adam is to blame"? If someone wickedly slandered me, would I say, "This person is to be pitied, for he was born into the world with this evil disposition"? If someone whom I had always treated honorably and generously returned my kindness by doing all he could to injure me, and then said, "I could not help hating you," far from accepting that as a valid extenuation, I would rightly consider that his enmity made him all the more to blame.

When a sinner is truly awakened, humbled and broken before God, he realizes that he deserves to be damned for his vile rebellion against God, and freely acknowledges that he is what he is voluntarily and not by compulsion. He realizes that he has had no love for God, nor any desire to love Him. He admits that he is an enemy to Him in his very heart, and voluntarily so; that all his fair pretenses, promises, prayers and religious performances were mere hypocrisy, arising only from self-love, guilty fears and mercenary hopes. He feels himself to be without excuse and owns that eternal judgment is His just due. When truly convicted of sin by the Holy Spirit, the sinner is driven out of all his false refuges and owns that his inability is a criminal one, that he is guilty.

Chapter 4
Root

As no heart can sufficiently conceive, so no voice or pen can adequately portray the awful state of wretchedness and woe into which sin has cast guilty man. It has separated him from God and so has severed him from the only Source of holiness and true happiness. It has ruined him in spirit and soul and body. By the fall man not only plunged himself into a state of infinite guilt from which there is no deliverance unless sovereign grace unites him with the Mediator; by his apostasy man also lost his holiness and is wholly corrupt and under the dominion of dispositions or lusts which are directly contrary to God and His law (Rom. 8:7). The fall has brought man into love of sin and hatred of God. The corruption of man's being is so great and so entire that he will never truly repent or even have any right responses toward God and His law unless and until he is supernaturally renewed by the Holy Spirit.

Corruption of Human Nature

If any reader is inclined to think we have painted too dark a picture or have exaggerated the case of the fallen creature, we ask him to carefully ponder the second half of Romans 7 and note how human nature is there represented as so totally depraved as to be utterly unable not merely to keep God's law perfectly, but to do anything agreeable with it. "The law is spiritual: but I am carnal, sold under sin. For I know that in me (that is, in my flesh,) dwelleth no good thing: for to will is present with me; but how to perform that which is good I find not. But I see another law in my members, warring against the law of my mind, and bringing me into captivity to the law of sin which is in my members" (vv. 14, 18, 23). How completely at variance is that language from the sentiments which prevail in Christendom today. Paul, that most eminent Christian, nothing behind the chief apostles, when he considered what he was in himself, confessed that he was "sold under sin."

The apostle's phrase "in my flesh," as may be seen by tracing it through the New Testament, means "in me by nature." He was saying, "There is nothing in me naturally good." But before proceeding further let us seek to carefully define what is signified by the term "the natural man," or "man by nature." It does not mean the human nature itself, or man as a tripartite being of spirit and soul and body, for then we should include the Lord Jesus Christ, who truly and really assumed human nature, becoming the Son of Man. No, this term connotes not man as created, but man as corrupted. God did not in creation plant in us a principle of contrariety to Himself, for He fashioned man after His own image and likeness. He made him upright, holy. It was our defection from Him which plunged us into such immeasurable wretchedness and woe, which polluted and defiled all the springs of our being and corrupted all our faculties.

As a result of the fall man is the inveterate enemy of God, not only because of what he does, but because of what he now is in himself. Stephen Charnock said:

What kind of enmity this is. First, I understand it of nature, not of actions only. Every action of a natural man is an enemy's action, but not an action of enmity. A toad doth not envenom every spire of grass it crawls upon nor poison everything it toucheth, but its nature is poisonous. Certainly every man's nature is worse than his actions: as waters are purest at the fountain, and poison most pernicious in the mass, so is enmity in the heart. And as waters partake of the mineral vein they run through, so the actions of a wicked man are tinctured with the enmity they spring from, but the mass and strength of this is lodged in his nature. There is in all our natures such a diabolical contrariety to God, that if God should leave a man to the current of his own heart, it would overflow in all kinds of wickedness.

It is quite true that their deep enmity against God is less openly displayed by some than others, but this is not because they are any better in themselves than those who cast off all pretenses of decency. Their moderation in wickedness is to be attributed to the greater restraints which God places upon them either by the secret workings of His Spirit upon their hopes and fears or by His external providences—such as education, religious instruction, the subduing influence of the pious. But none is born into this world with the slightest spark of love to God in him. "The wicked are estranged from the womb: they go astray as soon as they be born, speaking lies. Their poison is like the poison of a serpent" (Ps. 58:3-4). The poison of a serpent is radically the same in all of its species.

"That which is born of the flesh is flesh" (John 3:6). These words make it clear that inherent corruption is imparted to us by birth. This is evident from the remainder of the verse: "and that which is born of the Spirit is spirit." The "spirit" which is begotten differs from the Spirit who is the Begetter, and signifies that new creation of holiness which is effected and inbred in the soul and therefore is called "the seed of God" (1 John 3:9). As the spirit here unquestionably denotes the new nature or principle of holiness, so the flesh in John 3:6 stands for the old nature or principle of sin. This is further established by Galatians 5:17: "For the flesh lusteth against the Spirit, and the Spirit against the flesh: and these are contrary the one to the other: so that ye cannot do the things that ye would." Flesh and spirit are there put as two inherent qualities conveyed by two several births, and so are in that respect opposed. That the flesh refers to our very nature as corrupt is seen from the fact that it has works or fruits. The flesh is a principle from which operations issue, as buds from a root.

The scope of Christ in John 3 shows that flesh has reference to the corruption of our nature. His evident design in those verses was to show what imperative need there is for fallen man to be regenerated. Now regeneration is nothing else but a working of new spiritual dispositions in the whole man, called there "spirit," without which it is impossible that he should enter the kingdom of God. Christ said, "That which is born of the flesh is flesh" (v. 6), by which statement He made it the direct opposite of the spirit of holiness which is wrought in the soul by the Holy Spirit. Had we derived only guilt from Adam we would need only justification; but since we also derived corruption of nature we need regeneration too.

There is, then, in every man born into this world a mass of corruption which inheres in and clings to him and which is the principle and spring of all his activities. This may justly be termed his nature, for it is the predominant quality which is in all and which directs all that issues from him. Let us now proceed to the proof of this compound assertion. First, it is a mass of corruption, for that which our Lord called flesh in John 3:6 is called "the old man, which is corrupt" by His apostle in Ephesians 4:22. Observe carefully what is clearly implied by this term, and see again how perfectly one part of Scripture harmonizes with another. Corruption necessarily denotes something which was previously good, and so it is with man. God made him righteous; now he is defiled. Instead of having a holy soul, it is depraved; instead of an immortal body, it has within it even now the seeds of putrefaction.

Second, we have said that this corruption cleaves to man's very nature. It is expressly said to be within him: "Now then it is no more I that do it, but sin that dwelleth in me. For I know that in me (that is, in my flesh,) dwelleth no good thing" (Rom. 7:17-18). Man, then, has not only acts of sin which are transient, which come from him and go away, but he has a root and spring of sin dwelling with him, residing in him, not only adjacent to but actually inhabiting him. Not simply our ways and works are corrupt; "the heart is deceitful above all things, and desperately wicked" (Jer. 17:9). Nor is this something which we acquire through association with the wicked; rather it is that which we bring with us into the world: "Foolishness is bound in the heart of a child" (Prov. 22:15).

Third, we have stated that this indwelling corruption is the predominant principle of all the actions of unregenerate man, that from which all proceeds. Surely this is clear from "Now the works of the flesh are manifest, which are these: adultery, fornication, uncleanness, lasciviousness, idolatry, witchcraft, hatred, variance, emulations, wrath, strife" (Gal. 5:19-21). The flesh is here said to have works or fruits, and this quality of fruit-bearing exists in man's nature. Note that hatred and wrath are not deeds of the body, but dispositions of the soul and affections of the heart; thus the flesh cannot be restricted to our physical structure. This evil principle or corruption is divinely labeled a root: "Lest there should be among you a root that beareth gall and wormwood" (Deut. 29:18; cf. Heb. 12:13). It is a root which brings forth "gall and wormwood," that is, the bitter fruits of sin; in fact, it is said to "bring forth fruit unto death" (Rom. 7:5).

Fourth, we have affirmed that there is a mass of this corruption which thoroughly affects and defiles man's being. This is confirmed by the fact that in Colossians 2:11 it is called a body, which has many members: "In whom also ye are circumcised with the circumcision made without hands, in putting off the body of the sins of the flesh by the circumcision of Christ." This body of the sins of the flesh is of abounding dimensions, a body which has internal and external manifestations, gross and more secret lusts. Among these are atheism and contempt or hatred of God, which is not fully perceived by man until the Holy Spirit pierces him to the dividing asunder of soul and spirit. That this corruption lies in the very nature of man appears from the psalmist's statement "Behold, I was shapen in iniquity; and in sin did my mother conceive me" (51:5). David was there confessing the spring from which his great act of sin sprang. In essence he said, "I have not only committed the awful act of adultery, but there is sin even in my inward parts, defiling me from the moment I was conceived" (cf. v. 6).

Finally, we have declared that this corruption may in a very real sense be termed the nature of man. Once more we appeal to John 3:6 in proof, for there it is predicated in the abstract, which implies more than a simple quality, even that which explains the very definition and nature of man. The Lord Jesus did not say merely, "That which is born of the flesh is fleshly"; He said it "is flesh." In that statement Christ framed a new definition of man, beyond any the philosophers have framed. Philosophers define man as a rational animal; the Son of God announces him to be flesh, that is, sin and corruption contrary to grace and holiness, this being his very nature as a fallen creature in the sight of God. The very fact that this definition of man's nature is, as it were, in the abstract argues that it is a thing inherent in us. But let us enlarge a little on this point.

Definitions are taken from things brought out in nature, and none but essential properties are ingredients in definitions. Definitions are taken from the most predominant qualities. Sinful corruption is a more predominant principle in man's nature than is reason itself, for it not only guides reason, but it resides in every part and faculty of man, while reason does not. This corruption is so inbred and predominant and so diffused through the whole man that there is mutual expression between man and it. In John 3:6 the whole of man's nature is designated flesh; in Ephesians 4:22 this corruption is called man: "Put off . . . the old man, which is corrupt." Obviously we cannot put off our essential substance or discard our very selves, only that which is sinful and foul. It is called the old man because it is inherited from Adam, and because it is contrasted with our new nature.

Bondage of Corruption

Man's nature, then, which has become corrupt and termed flesh, is a bundle of foolishness and vileness, and it is this which renders him totally impotent to all that is good. Thus Scripture speaks of "the bondage of corruption" (Rom. 8:21) and declares men to be "the servants [Greek, 'slaves'] of corruption" (2 Pet. 2:19). Reluctant as any are to acknowledge this humbling truth, the solemn fact that the very nature of man is corrupt and that it defiles everything which issues from him is clearly and abundantly demonstrated. First, the human creature sins from earliest years. The first acts which evidence reason have sin also mingled with them. Take any child and observe him closely, and it will be found that the first dawnings of reason are corrupt. Children express reason selfishly—as in rebellion when thwarted, in readiness to please themselves, in doing harm to others, in excusing themselves by lying, in pride of apparel.

John Bunyan said:

To speak my mind freely: I do confess it is my opinion that children come polluted with sin into the world, and that oftentimes the sins of their youth—especially while they are very young—are rather by virtue of indwelling sin than by examples that are set before them by others: not but what they learn to sin by example too, but example is not the root but rather the temptation to wickedness.

How can we believe otherwise when our Lord has expressly affirmed, "For from within, out of the heart of .men [and not from association with degenerates], proceed evil thoughts, adulteries, fornications, murders, thefts, covetousness, wickedness, deceit, lasciviousness, an evil eye, blasphemy, pride, foolishness: all these things come from within, and defile the man" (Mark 7:21-23). It is true that evil habits may be acquired through contact with evildoers, but they are the occasion and not the radical cause of the habits.

This pollution of our very nature, this indwelling corruption, holds men in complete bondage, making them utterly impotent to do that which is good. In further proof of this, let us turn again to Romans 7. In his explanation of why he was unable to perform that obedience which God required, the apostle said, "I find then a law, that, when I would do good, evil is present with me. For I delight in the law of God after the inward man: but I see another law in my members, warring against the law of my mind, and bringing me into captivity to the law of sin which is in my members" (vv. 21-23). Indwelling sin is here called a law. Literally, a law is a moral rule which directs and commands, which is enforced with rewards and penalties, which impels its subjects to do the things ordered and to avoid the things forbidden. Figuratively, law is an inward principle that moves and inclines constantly to action. As the law of gravity draws all objects to their center, so sin is an effectual principle and power inclining to actions according to its own evil nature.

When the apostle says, "I see another law in my members" (that is, in addition to the principle of grace and holiness communicated at the new birth), he refers to the presence and being of indwelling sin; when he adds "bringing me into captivity" he signifies its power and efficacy. Indwelling sin is a law even in believers, though not to them. Paul said, "I find, then. . . a law of sin." It was a discovery which he had made as a regenerate man. From painful experience he found there was that in him which hindered his communion with God, which thwarted his deepest longings to live a sinless life. The operations of divine grace preserve in believers a constant and ordinarily prevailing will to do good, notwithstanding the power and efficacy of indwelling sin to the contrary. But the will in unbelievers is completely under the power of sin—their will of sinning is never taken away. Education, religion and convictions of conscience may restrain unbelievers, but they have no spiritual inclinations of will to do that which is pleasing to God.

That the very nature of man is corrupt, that it defiles everything which issues from him, is apparent not only by his sinning from earliest youth. Second, it is apparent by his sinning constantly. Not only is his first act sinful; all his subsequent actions are such. "And God saw that the wickedness of man was great in the earth, and that every imagination of the thoughts of his heart was only evil continually" (Gen. 6:5)—nor has man improved the slightest since then. Not that everything done by the natural man is in its own nature sinful; but as the acts are those of a sinner, they cannot be anything else than sinful. The act itself may be the performance of duty; yet if there is no respect for the commandment of God, it is sinful. To provide food and raiment is a duty, but if this duty is done from no spiritual motive (out of subjection to God's authority or the desire to please Him) or end (that God may be glorified), it is sinful. "The plowing of the wicked is sin" (Prov. 21:4); plowing is a duty in itself; nevertheless it is sinful as being the action of a sinner.

Third, it is not thus with a few, but with every member of Adam's fallen race. This further demonstrates that all evil proceeds from the very nature of man. "All flesh had corrupted his way upon the earth" (Gen. 6:12). "There is none righteous, no, not one. . . . They are all gone out of the way, they are together become unprofitable; there is none that doeth good" (Rom. 3:10-12). All members of the human race sin thus of their own accord. "A child left to himself bringeth his mother to shame" (Prov. 29:15). A child does not have to be taught to sin; he has only to be left to himself, and he will soon bring his parents to shame. Things which are not natural have to be taught us and diligently practiced before we learn them. Throw a child into the water, and it is helpless; throw an animal in, and it will at once begin to swim, for its nature teaches it to do so. "Train up a child in the way he should go" (Prov. 22:6). Much diligence and patience are required in those who would thus train the child; but no instructors are needed to inform him of the way in which he should not go. His depraved nature urges him into forbidden paths; indeed, it makes him delight in them.

Chapter 5
Extent

When seeking to uphold some other great truths of Scripture by means of contemplating separately their component parts, we reminded the reader how very difficult it was to avoid some overlapping. The same thing needs to be pointed out here in connection with the subject we are now considering. A river has many tributaries and a surveyor must necessarily trace out each one separately, yet he does so with the knowledge that they all run out of or into the same main stream. A tree has many boughs which, though distinct members of it, often interweave. So it is with our present theme, and as we endeavor to trace its various branches there is of necessity a certain measure of repetition. Though in one way this is to be regretted, being apt to weary the impatient, yet it has its advantages, for it better fixes in our minds some of the principal features.

We began by showing the solemn reality of man's spiritual impotence, furnishing clear proofs from Holy Writ. Next, we endeavored to delineate in detail the precise nature of man's inability: that it is penal, moral, voluntary and criminal. Then we considered the root of the awful malady, evidencing that it lies in the corruption of our very nature. We now examine the extent of the spiritual paralysis which has attacked fallen man's being. Let us state it concisely before elaborating and offering confirmation. The spiritual impotence of the natural man is total and entire, irreparable and irremediable as far as all human efforts are concerned. Fallen man is utterly indisposed and disabled, thoroughly opposed to God and His law, wholly inclined to evil. Sooner would thistles yield grapes than fallen man originate a spiritual volition.

Reign of Sin in Unregenerate

We have supplied a number of proofs that man's nature is now thoroughly corrupt. This is seen in the fact that he is sinful from his earliest years; the first dawnings of reason in a child are fouled by sin. It appears too in that men sin continually. As Jeremiah 13:23 expresses it, they are "accustomed to do evil." It is also evidenced by the universal prevalence of this disease; not only some, nor even the great majority, but all without exception are depraved. It is demonstrated by their freedom in this state. All sin continually of their own accord. A child has only to be left to himself and he will quickly put his mother to shame. Moreover, men cannot be restrained from their sin. Neither education nor religious instruction, neither expostulation nor threatening (human or divine) will deter them; that which is bred in the bone comes out in the flesh. Corruption can neither be eradicated nor moderated. The tongue is a little member, yet God Himself declares it is one which no man can tame (Jam. 3:8).

"The law of sin which is in my members" (Rom. 7:23). The first thing which attends every law as such is its rule or sway: "The law hath dominion over [literally 'lords it over'] a man as long as he liveth" (Rom. 7:1). The giving of law is the act of a superior, and in its very nature it exacts obedience by way of dominion. The law of sin possesses no moral authority over its subjects, but because it exerts a powerful and effectual dominion over its slaves it is rightly termed a law. Though it has no rightful government over men, yet it has the equivalent, for it dominates as a king: "Sin hath reigned unto death" (Rom. 5:21). Because believers have been delivered from the complete dominion of this evil monarch, they are exhorted, "Let not sin therefore reign in your mortal body, that ye should obey it in the lusts thereof" (Rom. 6:12). Here we learn the precise case with the unregenerate: Sin reigns undisputedly within them, and they yield ready and full obedience to it.

The second thing which attends all law as such is its sanctions, which have efficacy to move those who are under the law to do the things it requires. In other words, a law has rewards and penalties accompanying it, and these serve as inducements to obedience even though the things commanded are unpleasant. Speaking generally, all laws owe their efficacy to the rewards and punishments annexed to them. Nor is the "law of sin"—indwelling corruption—any exception. The pleasures and profits which sin promises its subjects are rewards which the vast majority of men lose their souls to obtain. A striking biblical illustration of this is the occasion when the law of sin contended against the law of grace in Moses, who chose "rather to suffer affliction with the people of God, than to enjoy the pleasures of sin for a season; esteeming the reproach of Christ greater riches than the treasures in Egypt: for he had respect unto the recompense of the reward" (Heb. 11:25-26).

In the above example we see the conflict in the mind of Moses between the law of sin and the law of grace. The motive on the part of the law of sin, by which it sought to influence him and with which it prevails over the majority, was the temporary reward which it set before him, namely, the present enjoyment of the pleasures of sin. By that it contended with the eternal reward annexed to the law of grace, called here "the recompense of the reward." By this wretched reward the law of sin keeps the whole world in obedience to its commands. Scripture, observation and personal experience teach us how powerful and potent this influence is. This was what induced our first parents to taste the forbidden fruit, Esau to sell his birthright, Balaam to hire himself to Balak, Judas to betray the Savior. This is what now moves the vast majority of our fellowmen to prefer Mammon to God, Belial to Christ, the things of time and sense to spiritual and eternal realities.

The law of sin also has penalties with which it threatens any who are urged to cast off its yoke. These are the sneers, the ostracism, the persecutions of their peers. The law of sin announces to its votaries that nothing but unhappiness and suffering is the portion of those who would be in subjection to God, that His service is oppressive and joyless. It represents the yoke of Christ as a grievous burden, His gospel as quite unsuited to those who are young and healthy, the Christian life as a gloomy and miserable thing. Whatever troubles and tribulations come on the people of God because of their fidelity to Him, whatever hardships and self-denial the duties of mortification require, are represented by the law of sin as so many penalties following the neglect of its commands. By these it prevails over the "fearful, and unbelieving," who have no share in the life eternal (Rev. 21:8). It is hard to say where its greater strength lies: in its pretended rewards or in its pretended punishments.

The power and effect of this law of sin appears from its very nature. It is not an outward, inoperative, directing law, but an inbred, working, effectual law. A law which is proposed to us cannot be compared for efficacy with a law bred in us. God wrote the moral law on tables of stone, and now it is found in the Scriptures. But what is its efficacy? As it is external to men and proposed to them, does it enable them to perform the things which it requires? No indeed. The moral law is rendered "weak through the flesh" (Rom. 8:3). Indwelling corruption makes it impossible for man to meet its demands. And how does God deliver from this awful bondage? In this present life by making His law internal for His elect, for at their regeneration He makes good that promise "I will put my law in their inward parts, and write it in their hearts" (Jer. 31:33). Thus His law becomes an internal, living, operative and effectual principle within them.

Now the law of sin is an indwelling law. It is "sin that dwelleth in me"; it is "in my members." It is so deep in man that in one sense it is said to be the man himself: "I know that in me (that is, in my flesh,) there dwelleth no good thing" (Rom. 7:18; cf. vv. 20, 23). From this reasoning we may perceive the full dominion it has over the natural man. It always abides in the soul, and is never absent. It "dwelleth," has its constant residence, in us. It does not come upon the soul only at certain times; if that were so, much might be accomplished during its absence, and the soul might fortify itself against it. No, it never leaves. Wherever we are, whatever we are engaged in, this law of sin is present. Whether we are alone or in company, by night or by day, it is our constant companion. A ruthless enemy indwells our soul. How little this is considered by men! O the woeful security of the unregenerate: a fire is in their bones, fast consuming them. The watchfulness of most professing Christians corresponds little to the danger of their state.

Being an indwelling law, sin applies itself to its work with great facility and ease. It needs not force open any door nor use any stress whatever. The soul cannot apply itself to any duty except by those very faculties in which this law has its residence. Let the mind or understanding be directed to anything, and there are ignorance, darkness, madness to contend with. As for the will, in it are spiritual deadness, mulish stubbornness, devilish obstinacy. Shall the affections of the heart be set on divine objects? How can they be, when they are wholly inclined toward the world and present things and are prone to every vanity and defilement? Water never rises above its own level. How easy it is, then, for indwelling sin to inject itself into all we do, hindering whatever is good and furthering whatever is evil. Does conscience seek to assert itself? Then our corruptions soon teach us to turn a deaf ear to its voice.

The Scripture everywhere declares the seat of this law of sin to be the heart. "Out of the heart are the issues of life" (Prov. 4:23). It is there that indwelling corruption keeps its special residence; it is there this evil monarch holds court. It has invaded and possessed the throne of God within us. "The heart of the sons of men is full of evil, and madness is in their heart while they live" (Eccles. 9:3). Here is the source of all the madness which appears in men s lives. "All these evil things [mentioned in vv. 21-22] come from within, and defile the man" (Mark 7:23). There are many outward temptations and provocations which befall man, which excite and stir him up to many evils; yet they merely open the vessel and let out what is stored within it. "An evil man out of the evil treasure of his heart bringeth forth that which is evil: for of the abundance of the heart his mouth speaketh" (Luke 6:45). This "evil treasure" or store is the principle of all moral action on the part of the natural man. Temptations and occasions put nothing into men; they only draw out what was in them before. The root or spring of all wickedness lies in the center of our corrupt being.

Enmity of Carnal Mind Against God

Let us next consider the outstanding property of indwelling sin. "The carnal mind is enmity against God: for it is not subject to the law of God, neither indeed can be" (Rom. 8:7). That which is here called the carnal mind is the same as the law of sin. It is to be solemnly noted that the carnal mind is not only an enemy, for as such there would be a possibility of some reconciliation with God; it is enmity itself, thus not disposed to accept any terms of peace. Enemies may be reconciled, but enmity cannot. The only way to reconcile enemies is to destroy their enmity. So the apostle tells us, "When we were enemies, we were reconciled to God by the death of his Son" (Rom. 5:10); that is, a supernatural work has been accomplished in the elect on the ground of the merits of Christ's sacrifice, which results in the reconciliation of those who were enemies. But when the apostle came to speak of enmity there was no other way but for it to be destroyed: "Having abolished in his flesh the enmity" (Eph. 2:15).

Let it also be duly considered that the apostle used a noun and not an adjective: "The carnal mind is enmity against God" (Rom. 8:7). He did not say that it merely is opposed to God, but that it is positive opposition itself. It is not black but blackness; it is not an enemy but enmity; it is not corrupt but corruption itself; not rebellious but rebellion. As C. H.

Spurgeon so succinctly expressed it, "The heart, though it be deceitful, is positively deceitful: it is evil in the concrete, sin in the essence: it is the distillation, the quintessence of all things that are vile; it is not envious against God, it is enmity itself—not at enmity, it is actual enmity." This is unspeakably dreadful. To the same effect are those fearful words of the psalmist: "Their inward part is very wickedness" (5:9). Beyond that human language cannot go.

This carnal mind is in every fallen creature, not even excluding the newborn infant. Many who have had the best of parents have turned out the worst of sons and daughters. This carnal mind is in each of us every moment of our lives. It is there just as truly when we are unconscious of its presence as when we are aware of the rising of opposition in us to God. The wolf may sleep, but it is a wolf still. The snake may rest among the flowers, and a boy may stroke its back, but it is a snake still. The sea is the house of storms even when it is placid as a lake. And the heart, when we do not see its seethings, when it does not spew out the hot lava of its corruption, is still the same dread volcano.

The extent of this fearful enmity appears in the fact that the whole of the carnal mind is opposed to God: every part, every power, every passion of it. Every faculty of man's being has been affected by the fall. Take the memory. Is it not a solemn fact that we retain evil things far more easily than those which are good? We can recollect a foolish song much more readily than we can a passage of Scripture. We grasp with an iron hand things which concern our temporal interests, but hold with feeble fingers those which respect our eternal welfare. Take the imagination. Why is it that when a man is given that which intoxicates him, or when he is drugged with opium, his imagination soars as on eagles' wings? Why does not the imagination work thus when the body is in a normal condition? Simply because it is depraved; and unless our body enters a sordid environment the fancy will not hold high carnival. Take the judgment. How vain—often mad—are its reasonings even in the wisest of men.

This fearful enmity is irremediable. "It is not subject to the law of God, neither indeed can be" (Rom. 8:7). Even though divine grace intervenes and subdues its force, yet it does not affect the slightest change in its nature. It may not be so powerful and effectual in operation as when it had more life and freedom, yet it is enmity still. As every drop of poison is poison and will infect, as every spark of fire is fire and will burn, so is every part and degree of the law of sin enmity—it will poison, it will burn. The Apostle Paul can surely be regarded as having made as much progress in the subduing of this enmity as any man on earth, yet he exclaimed, "O wretched man that I am!" (Rom. 7:24) and cried for deliverance from this irreconcilable enmity. Mortification abates its awful force, but it does not affect any reformation in it. Whatever effect divine grace may work upon it, no change is made in it; it is enmity still.

Not only is this awful enmity inbred in every one of Adam's fallen race, not only has it captured and dominated every faculty of our beings, not

only is it present within us every moment of our lives, not only is it incapable of reconciliation. Most frightful of all, this indwelling sin is "enmity
against God." In other passages it is exhibited as our own enemy: "Abstain from fleshly lusts, which war against the soul" (1 Pet. 2:11): those
indwelling corruptions are constantly seeking to destroy us. This deadly
poison of sin, this ruinous law of indwelling evil, consistently opposes the
new nature or law of grace and holiness in the believer: "The flesh lusteth
against the Spirit" (Gal. 5:17); that is, the principle of sin fights against
and seeks to vanquish the principle of spirituality. It is dreadful to relate
that its proper formal object is God Himself. It is "enmity against God."

This frightful enmity has, as it were, received from Satan the same
command which the Assyrians had from their monarch: "Fight neither
with small nor great, save only with the king" (1 Kings 22:31). Sin sets
itself not against men but against the King of heaven. This appears in the
judgments which men form of God. What is the natural man's estimate of
the Creator and Ruler of this world? For answer let us turn to the regions
of heathendom. Consider the horrible superstitions, the disgusting rites,
the hideous symbols of Deity, the cruel penances and gross immoralities
which everywhere prevail in lands without the gospel. Consider the appalling abominations which for so long passed, and which in numerous
instances still pass, under the sacred name of divine worship. These are
not merely the products of ignorance of God; they are the immediate
fruits of positive enmity against Him.

But we need not go so far afield as heathendom. The same terrible feature confronts us in so-called Christendom. Witness the multitudinous
and horrible errors which prevail on every side in the religious realm today, the degrading and insulting views of the Most High held by the great
majority of church members. And what of the vast multitudes who make
no profession at all? Some think of and act toward the great Jehovah as
One who is to be little regarded and respected. They consider Him as One
entitled to very little esteem, scarcely worthy of any notice at all. "Therefore they say unto God, Depart from us, for we desire not the knowledge
of thy ways. What is the Almighty, that we should serve him? And what
profit should we have, if we pray unto him?" (Job 21:14-15). Such is the
language of their hearts and lives, if not of their lips. Countless others
flatly deny the existence of God.

The most solemn and dreadful aspect of the subject we are here contemplating is that the outstanding property of the "flesh" or indwelling
sin consists of enmity against God Himself, such enmity that "is not
subject to the law of God, neither indeed can be" (Rom. 8:7). This frightful and implacable enmity is entire and universal, being opposed to all
of God. If there were anything of God—His nature, His character or His
works—that indwelling corruption was not enmity against, then the soul
might have a retreat within itself where it could shelter and apply itself
to that which is of God. Unfortunately, such is the enmity of fallen man
that it hates all that is of God, everything wherein or whereby we have to

do with Him.

Sin is enmity against God, and therefore against all of God. It is enmity against His law and against His gospel alike, against every duty to Him, against any communion with Him. It is not only against His sovereignty, His holiness, His power, His grace, that sin rears its horrible head; it abhors everything of or pertaining to God. His commandments and His threatenings, His promises and His warnings, are equally disliked. His providences are reviled and His dealings with the world blasphemed. And the nearer anything approaches to God, the greater is man's enmity against it. The more of spirituality and holiness manifested in anything, the more the flesh rises up against it. That which is most of God meets with most opposition. "Ye have set at naught all my counsel and would none of my reproof" (Prov. 1:25) is the divine indictment. The wicked heart of man is opposed to not merely some parts of God's counsel but the whole of it.

Not only is this fearful enmity opposed to everything of God, but it is all-inclusive in the soul. Had indwelling sin been content with partial dominion, had it subjugated only a part of the soul, it might have been more easily and successfully opposed. But this enmity against God has invaded and captured the entire territory of man's being; it has not left a single faculty of the soul free from its tyrannical yoke; it has not ex-empted a single member from its cruel bondage. When the Spirit of God comes with His gracious power to conquer the soul, He finds nothing whatever in the sinner's soul which is in sympathy with His operations, nothing that will cooperate with Him. All within us alike opposes and strives against His working. There is not the faintest desire for deliver-ance within the unregenerate: "The whole head is sick, and the whole heart faint" (Isa. 1:5). Even when grace has made its entrance, sin still dwells in all its coasts.

Distasteful and humiliating as this truth may be, we must dwell fur-ther on it and amplify what has been merely affirmed. We showed how this fearful enmity is evidenced by the judgments or concepts which men form of God. Sin has so perverted the human mind that distorted views and horrible ideas are entertained of the Deity. Nor is this all. Sin has so inflated the creature that he considers himself competent to comprehend the incomprehensible. Filled with pride, he refuses to acknowledge his limitations and dependence; and in his flight after things which are far beyond his reach, he indulges in the most impious speculations. When he cannot stretch himself to the infinite dimensions of truth, he delib-erately contracts the truth to his own little measure. This is what the apostle meant by fallen man's "vanity of mind."

The natural man's enmity against God appears in his affections. As the superlatively excellent One, God has paramount claims on man's heart. He should be the supreme object of his delight. But is He? Far from it. The smallest trifles are held in greater esteem than is God, the fountain of all true joy. The unregenerate see in Him no beauty that they should desire Him. When they hear of His sublime attributes they dislike them. When they hear His Word quoted it is repugnant to them. When invited to draw near to His throne of grace they have no inclination to do so. They have no desire for fellowship with God; they would rather think and talk about anything other than the Lord and His government. They secretly hate His people, and will only tolerate their presence so long as they conform to their wishes. The pleasures and baubles of this world entirely fill their hearts. Corrupted nature can never give birth to a single affection which is really spiritual.

The natural man's enmity appears in his will. Inevitably so, for God's will directly crosses His. God is infinitely holy; man is thoroughly evil; therefore God commands the things which man hates and forbids the things man likes. Hence man despises His authority, refuses His yoke, rebels against His government and goes his own way. Men have no concern for God's glory and no respect for His will. They will not listen to His reproofs nor be checked in their defiant course by His most solemn threatenings. They are as intractable as a wild ass' colt. They are like a bullock unaccustomed to the yoke. They prate of the freedom of their wills, but their wills are active against God and never toward Him. They are determined to have their own way no matter what the cost. When Christ is presented to them they will not come to Him that they might have life. Sooner will water flow uphill of its own accord than the will of man incline itself to God.

The enmity of the natural man against God appears in his conscience. Because he is anxious to be at peace with himself in the reflections which he makes upon his own life and character, it is obvious that his conscience must be a perpetual source of false representations of God. When guilt rankles in his breast, man will blaspheme the justice of his Judge. And self-love prompts him to denounce the punishment of himself as remorseless cruelty. A guilty conscience, unwilling to relinquish its iniquities and yet desirous of being delivered from fears of punishment, prompts men to represent Deity as subject to the weaknesses and follies of humanity. God is to be flattered and bribed with external marks of submission and esteem, or else insulted when the worshiper regards Him as cruel. Conscience fills the mind with prejudices against the nature and character of God, just as a human insult fills our heart with prejudice against the one who mortifies our self-respect. Conscience cannot judge rightly of one whom it hates and dreads.

The enmity of the natural man against God evidences itself in his practice. This dreadful hatred of God is not a passive thing, but an active principle. Sinners are involved in actual warfare against their Maker. They have enlisted under the banner of Satan and they deliberately oppose and defy the Lord. They scoff at His Word, disregard His precepts, flout His providences, resist His Spirit, and turn a deaf ear to the pleas of His servants. Their hearts are fully set to do wickedness. "Their throat is an open sepulcher; with their tongues they have used deceit: the poison of asps is under their lips: Whose mouth is full of cursing and bitterness: Their feet are swift to shed blood: destruction and misery are in their ways: and the way of peace have they not known: there is no fear of God before their eyes" (Rom. 3:13-18). There is in every sinner a deeply rooted aversion for God, a seed of malice. While God leaves sinners alone, their malice may not be clearly revealed; but let them feel a little of His wrath upon them, and their hatred is swiftly manifest.

The sinner's enmity against God is unmixed with any love at all. The natural man is utterly devoid of the principle of love for God. As Jonathan Edwards solemnly expressed it, "The heart of the sinner is as devoid of love for God as a corpse is of vital heat." As the Lord Jesus expressly declared, "I know you, that ye have not the love of God in you" (John 5:42). And remember, that fearful indictment was made by One who could infallibly read the human heart. Moreover that indictment was passed on not the openly vicious and profane but on the strictest religionists of His day. Reader, you may have a mild temper, an amiable disposition, a reputation for kindness and generosity; but if you have never been born again you have no more real love in your heart for God than Judas had for the Savior. What a frightful character—the unmitigated enemy of God!

The power of man's enmity against God is so great that nothing finite can break it. The sinner cannot break it himself. Should an unregenerate person read this and be horrified at the hideous picture which it presents of himself, and should he earnestly resolve to cease his vile enmity against God, he cannot do so. He can no more change his nature than the Ethiopian can change the color of his skin. No preacher can persuade him to throw down the weapons of his rebellion and become a friend of God. One may set before him the excellence of the divine character and plead with him to be reconciled to God, but his heart will remain as steeled against Him as ever. Even though God Himself works miracles in the sight of sinners, no change is effected in their hearts. Pharaoh's enmity was not overcome by the most astonishing displays of divine power, nor was that of the religionists of Palestine in Christ's day.

Indwelling sin may be likened to a powerful and swiftly flowing river. So long as its tributaries are open and waters are continually supplied to its streams, though a dam is set up, its waters rise and swell until it bears down on all and overflows the banks about it. Thus it is with the enmity of the carnal mind against God. While its springs and fountains remain open, it is utterly vain for man to set up a dam of his convictions and resolutions, promises and penances, vows and self-efforts. They may check it for a while, but it will rise up and rage until sooner or later it breaks down all those convictions and resolutions or makes itself an underground passage by some secret lust which will give full vent to it. The springs of that enmity must be subdued by regenerating grace, the streams abated by holiness, or the soul will be drowned and destroyed. Even after regeneration, indwelling sin gives the soul no rest, but constantly wages war upon it.

The Christian is, in fact, the only one who is conscious of the awful power and ragings of this principle of enmity. How often he is made aware that when he would do good, evil is present with him, opposing every effort he makes Godward. How often, when his soul is doing quite another thing, engaged in a totally different design, sin starts something in his heart or imagination which carries it away to that which is evil. Yes, the soul may be seriously engaged in the mortification of sin, when indwelling corruption will by some means or other lead the soul into trifling with the very sin which it is endeavoring to conquer. Such surprisals as these are proofs of the habitual propensity to evil of that principle of enmity against God from which they proceed. The ever abiding presence and continual operation of this principle prevent much communion with God, disturb holy meditations and defile the conscience.

But let us return to our consideration of the enmity of the unregenerate. This enmity in the heart of the sinner is so great that he is God's mortal enemy. Now a man may feel unfriendly toward another, or he may cherish ill will against him, yet not be his mortal enemy. That is, his enmity against the one he hates is not so great that nothing will satisfy him but his death. But it is far otherwise with sinners and God. They are His mortal enemies. True, it does not lie in their power to kill Him, yet the desire is there in the heart. There is a principle of enmity within fallen man which would rejoice if Deity could be annihilated. "The fool hath said in his heart, There is no God" (Ps. 14:1). In the Bible the words "there is" are in italics—supplied by the translators for clarity. But the original has it, "The fool hath said in his heart, No God." It is not the denial of God's existence, but the affirmation that he desires no contact with Him: "I desire no God; I would that He did not exist."

Here is the frightful climax: The carnal mind is enmity with the very being of God. Sin is destructive of all being. Man is suicidal—he has destroyed himself. He is homicidal—his evil influence destroys his fellowmen. He is guilty of Deicide(the act of killing a divine being)—he wishes he could annihilate the very being of God. But the sinner does not regard himself as being so vile. He does not consider himself to be the implacable and inveterate enemy of God. He has a far better opinion of himself than that. Consequently, if he hears or reads anything like this, he is filled with objections: "I do not believe I am such a dreadful creature as to hate God. I do not feel such enmity in my heart. I am not conscious that I harbor any ill will against Him. Who should know better than myself? If I hate a fellowman I am aware of it; how could I be totally unconscious of it if there is in my soul such enmity against God?"

Several answers may be given to these questions. First, if the objector would seriously examine his heart and contemplate himself, unless he were strangely blinded, he would certainly discover in himself those very elements in which enmity essentially consists. He loves and respects his friends, he is fond of their company, he is anxious to please them and promote their good. Is this his attitude toward God? If he is honest with himself, he knows it is not. He has no respect for His authority, no concern for His glory, no desire for fellowship with Him. He gives God none of his time, despises His Word, breaks His commandments, rejects His Son. He has been opposed to God all his life. These things are the very essence of enmity.

Second, the sinner's ignorance and unconsciousness of his enmity against God are due to the false conceptions which he entertains of His nature and character. If he were better acquainted with the God of Holy Writ, he would be more aware of his hatred of Him. But the God he believes in is merely a creation of his own fancy. The true God is ineffably holy, inflexibly just. His wrath burns against sin and He will by no means clear the guilty. If mankind likes the true God, why is it that they have set up so many false gods? If they admire the truth, why have they invented so many false systems of religion? The contrariety between the carnal mind and God is the contrariety between sin and holiness. The divine law requires man to love God supremely; instead, he loves himself supremely. It requires him to delight in God superlatively; instead, he wholly delights in all that is not of God. It requires him to love his neighbor as himself; instead, his heart is inordinately selfish.

Third, we have said that the enmity of the natural man against God is a mortal one. This the sinner will not admit. But indubitable proof of the assertion is found in man's treatment of God when, in the person of His Son, He became incarnate. When God brought Himself as near to man as Infinity could approach, man saw in Him "no beauty" that he should desire Him; rather was He despised and rejected by him. Not only did man dislike Him (Isa. 53:2-3), but he hated Him "without a cause" (John 15:25). So bitter and relentless was that hatred that man exclaimed, "This is the heir: come, let us kill him" (Luke 20:14). And what form of death did man select for Him? The most painful and shameful his malignity could devise. And the Son of God is still despised and rejected. Remember His words "He that hateth me hateth my Father also" (John 15:23). Our proof is complete.

What bearing on our subject has this lengthy discourse on man's enmity? Why take up the total depravity of fallen man when we are supposed to be considering his spiritual impotence? We have not wandered from our theme at all. Instead, while dealing with the root and extent of man's impotence, we have followed strictly the order of Scripture. What is the very next word of the apostle's after Romans 8:7? This: "So then they that are in the flesh cannot please God" (v. 8). It is just because man is corrupt at the very center of his being, because indwelling sin is a law over him, because his mind (the noblest part of his being) is enmity against God, that he is completely incapable of doing anything to meet with the divine approbation.

Here is inevitable inference, the inescapable conclusion: "So then"—because fallen man's mind is enmity with God and incapable of subordination to His law—"they that are in the flesh cannot please God" (Rom. 8:8). To be "in the flesh" is not necessarily to live immorally, for there is the religiousness as well as the irreligiousness of the flesh. So great, so entire, so irremediable is this impotence of fallen man that he is unable to effect any change in his nature, acquire any strength by his own efforts, prepare himself to receive divine grace, until the Spirit renews him and works in him both to will and to do of God's good pleasure. He is unable to discern spiritual things (1 Cor. 2:14), incapable of believing (John 8:47), powerless to obey (Rom. 8:7). He cannot think a good thought of himself (2 Cor. 3:5), he cannot speak a good word; indeed, without Christ he "can do nothing" (John 15:5). Thus, the sinner is "without strength," wholly impotent and unable to turn himself to God.

Chapter 6
Problem

We have now arrived at the most difficult part of our subject, and much wisdom from above is needed if we are to be preserved from error. It has been well said that truth is like a narrow path running between two precipices. The figure is an apt one, for fatal consequences await those who depart from the teaching of God's Word, no matter which direction that departure may take. It is so with the doctrine of man's impotence. It matters little whether the total bondage of the fallen creature and his utter inability to perform that which is good in the sight of God are repudiated and the freedom of the natural man is insisted on, or whether his complete spiritual impotence is affirmed and at the same time his responsibility to perform that which is pleasing to God is denied. In either case the effect is equally disastrous. In the former, the sinner is given a false confidence; in the latter, he is reduced to fatalistic inertia. In either case the real state of man is grossly misrepresented.

Man's Inability and God's Demands

The careful reader must have felt the force of the difficulties which we shall now examine. May God's Spirit enable us to throw some light on them. If the carnal mind is such fearful enmity against God that it is not subject to His law, "neither indeed can be," then why does He continue to press its demands on us and insist that we meet its requirements under pain of eternal death? If the fall has left man morally helpless and reduced him to the point where he is "without strength," then with what propriety can he be called on to obey the divine precepts? If man is so thoroughly depraved that he is the slave of sin, wherein lies his accountability to live for the glory of God? If man is born under "the bondage of corruption," how can he possibly be "without excuse" in connection with the sins he commits?

In seeking to answer these and similar questions we must of necessity confine ourselves to what is clearly revealed on them in Holy Writ. We say "of necessity," for unless we forsake our own thoughts (Isa. 55:7) and completely submit our minds to God's, we are certain to err. In theory this is granted by most professing Christians, yet in practice it is too often set aside. In general it is conceded, but in particular it is ignored. A highly trained intellect may draw what appear to be incontestable conclusions from a scriptural premise; yet, though logic cannot refute them, the practices of Christ and His apostles prove them to be false. On the one hand we may take the fact that the Lord has given orders for His gospel to be preached to every creature. Then must we not infer that the sinner has it in his own power to either accept or reject that gospel? Such an inference certainly appears reasonable, yet it is erroneous. On the other hand take the fact that the sinner is spiritually impotent. Then is it not a mockery to ask him to come to Christ? Such an inference certainly appears reasonable; yet it is false.

It is at this very point that most of Christendom has been deluged with a flood of errors. Most of the leading denominations began by taking the Word of God as the foundation and substance of their creed. But almost at once that foundation was turned into a platform on which the proud intellect of man was exercised, and in a very short time human reason— logical and plausible—supplanted divine revelation. Men attempted to work out theological systems and articles of faith that were thoroughly "consistent," theories which—unlike the workings of both nature and providence—contained in them no seeming "contradictions" or "absurdities," but which commended themselves to their fellowmen. But this was nothing less than a presumptuous attempt to compress the truth of God into man-made molds, to reduce that which issued from the Infinite to terms comprehensible to finite minds. It is another sad example of that egotism which refuses to receive what it cannot understand.

Biblical Harmony

It is true that there is perfect harmony in all parts of divine truth. How can it be otherwise, since God is its Author? Yet men are so blind that they cannot perceive this perfect harmony. Some cannot discern the consistency between the infinite love and grace of God and His requiring His own Son to pay such a costly satisfaction to His broken law. Some cannot see the consistency between the everlasting mercy of God and the eternal punishment of the wicked, insisting that if the former be true the latter is impossible. Some cannot see the congruity of Christ satisfying every requirement of God on behalf of His people and the imperative necessity of holiness and obedience in them if they are to benefit thereby; or between their divine preservation and the certainty of destruction were they to finally apostatize. Some cannot see the accord between the divine foreordination of our actions and our freedom in them. Some cannot see the agreement between efficacious grace in the conversion of sinners and the need for the exercise of their faculties by way of duty. Some cannot see the concurrence of the total depravity or spiritual impotence of man and his responsibility to be completely subject to God's will.

As a sample of what we have referred to in the last two paragraphs, note the following quotation:

We deny duty-faith, and duty-repentance—these terms signifying that it is every man's duty to spiritually and savingly repent and believe (Gen. 6:5; 8:21; Matt. 15:19; Jer. 17:9; John 6:44, 65). We deny also that there is any capability in man by nature to any spiritual good whatever. So that we reject the doctrine that men in a state of nature should be exhorted to believe in or turn to God (John 12:39, 40; Eph. 2:8; Rom. 8:7, 8; 1 Cor. 4:7). We believe that it would be unsafe, from the brief records we have of the way in which the apostles, under the immediate direction of the Lord, addressed their hearers in certain special cases and circumstances, to derive absolute and universal rules for ministerial addresses in the present day under widely-different circumstances. And we further believe that an assumption that others have been inspired as the apostles were has led to the grossest errors amongst both Romanists and professed Protestants. Therefore, that for ministers in the present day to address unconverted persons, or indiscriminately all in a mixed congregation, calling upon them to savingly repent, believe, and receive Christ, or perform any other acts dependent upon the new creative power of the Holy Ghost, is, on the one hand, to imply creature power and on the other, to deny the doctrine of special redemption.

It may come as a surprise to many of our readers to learn that the above is a verbatim quotation from the Articles of Faith of a Baptist group in England with a considerable membership, which will permit no man to enter their pulpits who does not solemnly subscribe to and sign his name to the same. Yet this is the case. These Articles of Faith accurately express the belief of the great majority of certain Baptist groups in the United States on this subject. In consequence, the gospel of Christ is deliberately withheld from the unsaved, and no appeals are addressed to them to accept the gospel offer and receive Christ as their personal Lord and Savior. Need we wonder that fewer and fewer in their midst are testifying to a divine work of grace in their hearts, and that many of their churches have ceased to be.

It is a good thing that many of the Lord's people are sounder of heart than the creeds held in their heads, yet that does not excuse them for subscribing to what is definitely unscriptural. It is far from a pleasant task to expose the fallacy of these Articles of Faith, for we have some friends who are committed to them; yet we would fail in our duty to them if we made no effort to convince them of their errors. Let us briefly examine these Articles. First, they deny that it is the duty of every man who hears the gospel to spiritually and savingly repent and believe, notwithstanding the fact that practically all the true servants of Christ in every generation (including the Reformers and nine-tenths of the Puritans) have preached that duty. It is the plain teaching of Holy Writ. We will not quote from the writings of those used of the Spirit in the past, but confine ourselves to God's Word.

God Himself "now commandeth all men everywhere to repent" (Acts 17:30). What could possibly be plainer than that? There is no room for any quibbling, misunderstanding or evasion. It means just what it says, and says just what it means. The framers of those Articles, then, are taking direct issue with the Most High. It is because of his "hardness and impenitence of heart" that the sinner treasures up to himself "wrath against the day of wrath" (Rom. 2:5). "He that believeth on him is not condemned: but he that believeth not is condemned already, because he hath not believed in the name of the only begotten Son of God. And this is the condemnation, that light is come into the world, and men loved darkness rather than light, because their deeds were evil" (John 3:18-19). Here too it is impossible to fairly evade the force of our Lord's language. He taught that it is the duty of all who hear the gospel to savingly believe on Him, and declared that rejecters are condemned because they do not believe. When He returns it will be "in flaming fire taking vengeance on them that know not God, and that obey not the gospel" (2 Thess. 1:8).

Next, note that the framers of these Articles follow their denial by referring to six verses of Scripture, the first four of which deal with the desperate wickedness of the natural man's heart and the last two with his complete inability to turn to Christ until divinely enabled. These passages are manifestly alluded to in support of the contention made. Each reader must decide their pertinence for himself. The only relevance they can possess is on the supposition that they establish a premise which requires us to draw the conclusion so dogmatically expressed. We are asked to believe that since fallen man is totally depraved we must necessarily infer that he is not a fit subject to be exhorted to perform spiritual acts. Thus, when analyzed, this Article is seen to consist of nothing more than an expression of human reasoning.

Not only does the substance of this Article of Faith consist of nothing more substantial and reliable than a mental inference, but when weighed in the balances of the sanctuary it is found to clash with the Scriptures, that is, with the practice of God's own servants recorded in them. For example, we do not find the psalmist accommodating his exhortations to the sinful inability of the natural man. Far from it. David called on the ungodly thus: "Be wise now therefore, O ye kings: be instructed, ye judges of the earth. Serve the Lord with fear, and rejoice with trembling. Kiss the Son, lest he be angry, and ye perish from the way, when his wrath is kindled but a little. Blessed are all they that put their trust in him" (Ps. 2:10-12). David did not withhold these warnings because the people were such rebels that they would not and could not give their hearts' allegiance to the King of kings. He uncompromisingly and bluntly commanded them to do so whether they could or not.

It was the same with the prophets. If ever a man addressed an unregenerate congregation it was when Elijah the Tishbite spoke to the idolatrous Israelites: "Elijah came unto all the people, and said, How long halt ye between two opinions? If the Lord be God, follow him: but if Baal, then follow him" (1 Kings 18:21). That exhortation was not restricted to the remnant of renewed souls, but was addressed to the nation indiscriminately. It was a plain call for them to perform a spiritual duty, for them to exercise their will and choose between God and the devil. In like manner Isaiah called on the debased generation of his day: "Wash ye, make you clean; put away the evil of your doings from before mine eyes; cease to do evil; learn to do well" (1:16-17). One prophet went so far as to say to his hearers, "Make you a new heart and a new spirit" (Ezek. 18:31), yet he was in perfect accord with his fellow prophet Jeremiah who taught the helplessness of man in those memorable questions "Can the Ethiopian change his skin? Or the leopard his spots?" These men, then, did not decide they must preach only that which lay in the power of their hearers to comply with.

The words "We deny also that there is any capability in man by nature to any spiritual good whatever" will strike the vast majority of God's people as far too sweeping. They will readily agree that fallen man possesses no power at all to perform any spiritual acts; yet they will insist that nothing prevents the spiritual obedience of any sinner except his own unwillingness. Man by nature—that is, as he originally left the hands of his Creator—was endowed with full capability to meet his Maker's requirements. The fall did not rob him of a single faculty, and it is his retention of all his faculties which constitutes him still a responsible creature. Of the last four passages referred to in the Article (John 12:39, 40, etc.) two of them relate to the spiritual impotence of fallen man and the other two to divine enablement imparted to those who are saved.

With regard to the other Articles affirming that it "would be unsafe" for us now to derive rules for ministerial address from the way in which the apostles spoke to their hearers, this is their summary method of disposing of all those passages in the Old and New Testaments alike which are directly opposed to their theory. Since the Lord Jesus Himself did not hesitate to say to the people, "Repent ye, and believe the gospel" (Mark 1:15), surely His servants today need not have the slightest hesitation in following His example. If ministers of the Word are not to find their guidance and rules from the practice of their Master and His apostles, then where shall they look for them? Must each one be a rule unto himself? Or must they necessarily place themselves under the domination of self-made popes? These very men who are such sticklers for "consistency" are not consistent with themselves, for when it comes to matters of church polity they take the practice of the apostles for their guidance! Lack of space prevents further comment on this.

To human reason there appears to be a definite conflict between two distinct lines of divine truth. On the one hand, Scripture plainly affirms that fallen man is totally depraved, enslaved by sin, entirely destitute of spiritual strength, so that he is unable of himself to either truly repent or savingly believe in Christ. On the other hand, Scripture uniformly addresses fallen man as a being who is accountable to God, responsible to forsake his wickedness and serve and glorify his Maker. He is called on to lay down the weapons of his warfare and be reconciled to God. The Ruler of heaven and earth has not lowered the standard of holiness under which He placed man. He declares that notwithstanding man's ruined condition, he is "without excuse" for all his iniquities. The gospel depicts man in a lost state, "dead in trespasses and sins"; nevertheless it exhorts all who come under its sound to accept Christ as their Lord and Savior.

Such in brief is the problem presented by the doctrine we are here considering. The unregenerate are morally impotent, yet are they fully accountable beings. They are sold under sin, yet are they justly required to be holy as God is holy. They are unable to comply with the righteous requirements of their Sovereign, yet they are exhorted to do so under pain of eternal death. What, then, should be our attitude to this problem? First, we should carefully test it and thoroughly satisfy ourselves that both of these facts are plainly set forth in Holy Writ. Second, having done so, we must accept them both at their face value, assured that however contrary they may seem to us, yet there is perfect harmony between all parts of God's Word. Third, we must hold firmly to both these lines of truth, steadfastly refusing to relinquish either of them at the dictates of any theological party or denominational leader. Fourth, we should humbly wait on God for fuller light on the subject.

But such a course is just what the proud heart of man is disinclined to follow. Instead, he desires to reduce everything to a simple, consistent and coherent system, one which falls within the compass of his finite understanding. Notwithstanding the fact that he is surrounded by mystery on every side in the natural realm, notwithstanding the fact that so very much of God's providential dealings both with the world in general and with himself in particular are "past finding out," he is determined to philosophize and manipulate God's truth until it is compressed into a series of logical propositions which appear reasonable to him. He is like the disciples whom our Lord called "fools" because they were "slow of heart to believe all that the prophets have spoken" (Luke 24:25). Those disciples were guilty of picking and choosing, believing what appealed to their inclination and rejecting that which was distasteful and which appeared to them to clash with what they had been taught.

Antinomian-Pelagian Debate

The testimony of the prophets did not seem to the disciples to be harmonious; one part appeared to conflict with another. In fact, there were two distinct lines of Messianic prediction which looked as though they flatly contradicted each other. The one spoke of a suffering, humiliated and crucified Messiah; the other of an all-powerful, glorious and triumphant Messiah. And because the disciples could not see how both could be true, they held to the one and rejected the other. Precisely the same capricious course has been followed by theologians in Christendom. Conflicting schools or parties among them have, as it were, divided the truth among themselves, one party retaining this portion and jettisoning that, and another party rejecting this and maintaining that. They have ranged themselves into opposing groups, each holding some facets of the truth, each rejecting what the opponents contend for. Party spirit has been as rife and as ruinous in the religious world as in the political.

On the one side Arminians have maintained that men are responsible creatures, that the claims of God are to be pressed upon them, that they must be called on to discharge their duty, that they are fit subjects for exhortation. Yet while steadfastly adhering to this side of the truth, they have been guilty of repudiating other aspects which are equally necessary and important. They have denied—in effect if not in words—the total depravity of man, his complete spiritual helplessness, the bondage of his will under sin, and his utter inability to cooperate with the Holy Spirit in the work of his salvation. On the other side Antinomians, while affirming all that the Arminians deny, are themselves guilty of repudiating what their opponents contend for, insisting that since the unregenerate have no power to perform spiritual acts it is useless and absurd to call on them to do so. Thus they aver that gospel offers should not be made unto the unregenerate.

These Antinomians consider themselves to be towers of orthodoxy, valiant defenders of the truth, sounder in the faith than any other section of Christendom. Many of them wish to be regarded as strict Calvinists; but whatever else they may be, they certainly are not that, for Calvin himself taught and practiced directly the contrary. In his work The Eternal Predestination of God the great Reformer wrote:

It is quite manifest that all men without difference or distinction are outwardly called or invited to repentance and faith; . . . the mercy of God is offered to those who believe and to those who believe not, so that those who are not Divinely taught within are only rendered inexcusable, not saved.

In his Secret Providence of God he asked:

And what if God invites the whole mass of mankind to come unto Him, and yet knowingly and of His own will denies His Spirit to the greater part, "drawing" a few only unto obedience unto Himself by His Spirit's secret inspiration and operation—is the adorable God to be charged, on that account, with inconsistency?

In the same work Calvin stated:

Nor is there any want of harmony or oneness of truth when the same Savior, who invites all men unto Him without exception by His external voice, yet declares that "A man can receive nothing except it be given him from above:" John 19:11.

Many regarding themselves as Calvinists have departed far from the teaching and practice of that eminent servant of God.

There is no difference in principle between the unregenerate being called on to obey the gospel and accept its gracious overtures, and the whole heathen world being required to respond to the call of God through nature before His Son became incarnate. In his address to the Athenians the apostle declared on Mars Hill, "God that made the world and all things therein, seeing that he is Lord of heaven and earth, dwelleth not in temples made with hands; neither is worshipped with men's hands, as though he needed anything, seeing he giveth to all life, and breath, and all things; and hath made of one blood all nations of men for to dwell on all the face of the earth, and hath determined the times before appointed, and the bounds of their habitation; that they should seek the Lord, if haply they might feel after him, and find him" (Acts 17:24-27). The force of that statement is this: Seeing God is the Creator, the Governor of all, He cannot be supposed to inhabit temples made by men, nor can He be worshiped with the products of their hands; and seeing that He is the universal Benefactor and Source of life and all things to His creatures, He is on that account required to be adored and obeyed; and since He is sovereign Lord appointing the different ages of the world and allotting to the nations their territories, His favor is to be sought after and His will submitted to.

The voice of nature is clear and loud. It testifies to the being of God and tells of His wisdom, goodness and power. It addresses all alike, bidding men to believe in God, turn to Him and serve Him. "The heavens declare the glory of God; and the firmament showed his handywork" (Ps. 19:1). These are the preachers of nature to all nations alike. They are not silent, but vocal, speaking to those in every land: "Day unto day uttereth speech, and night unto night showed knowledge. There is no speech nor language, where their voice is not heard. Their line is gone out through all the earth, and their words to the end of the world" (vv. 2-4). In view of these and similar phenomena the apostle declares, "That which may be known of God is manifest in them; for God hath showed it unto them. For the invisible things of him from the creation of the world are clearly seen, being understood by the things that are made, even his eternal power and Godhead; so that they are without excuse" (Rom. 1:19-20).

Now why do not Antinomians object to nature addressing men indiscriminately? Why do not these hyper-Calvinists protest against what we may designate the theology of the sun and the moon? Why do they not exclaim that there is no proper basis for such a call as nature makes? This view not only mocks the unregenerate, but belittles God, seeing that it is certain to prove fruitless, for He has not purposed that either savage or sage should respond to nature's call. But with the sober and the spiritual this branch of the divine government needs no apology. It is in all respects worthy of Him who is wonderful in counsel and excellent in working. Those groups of mankind who do not have the sacred Scriptures are as truly rational and accountable beings as those who are reared with God's written Word. Their having lost the power to read God's character in His works, as well as the inclination to seek after and find Him, does not in the least divest the Lord of His right to require of them both that inclination and power, and to deal with them by various methods of providence according to their several advantages.

It is altogether reasonable that intelligent creatures who, by falling into apostasy, have become blind to God's excellences and enemies to Him in their minds, should yet be commanded to yield Him the homage which is His due and should be urged and exhorted by a thousand tongues, speaking from every quarter of the heaven and the earth, to turn to Him as their supreme good, although it is absolutely certain that without gifts they do not possess, without a supernatural work of grace being wrought in their hearts, not one of them will ever incline his ear. Who does not perceive that this is an unimpeachable arrangement of things, in every respect worthy of the character of Him who is "righteous in all his ways, and holy in all his works" (Ps. 145:17)? The light of nature leaves all men without excuse, and God has a perfect right to require them to seek Him without vouchsafing the power of doing so, which power He is under no obligation to grant.

Exactly analogous to this is the case of those who come under the sound of the gospel, yet without being chosen to salvation or redemption by the precious blood of the Lamb. The love of God in Christ to sinners is proclaimed to them, and they are exhorted and entreated by all sorts of arguments to believe in Christ and be saved. Let it be clearly pointed out that no obstacle lies in the way of the reprobates' believing but what exists in their own evil hearts. Their minds are free to think and their wills to act. They do just as they please, unforced by anyone. They choose and refuse as seems good to themselves. The secret purpose of God in not appointing them to everlasting life or in withholding from them the renewing operations of His Spirit has no causal influence on the decision to which they come. Their advantages are vastly superior to the opportunities of those who enjoy only the light of nature.

The manifestation of the divine character granted to those living in Christendom is incomparably brighter and more impressive than that given to those born in heathendom, and consequently their responsibility is proportionately greater. Much more is given the former, and, on the ground of equity, much more will certainly be required of them (Luke 12:48). What, then, shall we say of the conduct of the Most High in His dealings with such persons? Shall we presumptuously question His sincerity in exhorting them by His Word or His sincerity in urging them by the general operations of His Spirit (Gen. 6:3; Acts 7:51)? With equal propriety we might question the sincerity of nature, when it bears witness to God's power in the shaking of the earth and the kindling of the volcano; or we might doubt God's goodness in clothing the valleys with corn and filling the pastures with flocks, leaving Himself "not . . . without witness" (Acts 14:17), in order that men "should seek the Lord, if haply they might feel after him, and find him" (Acts 17:27).

We by no means affirm that what we have pointed out entirely removes the difficulty felt by those who do not perceive the justice in exhorting sinners to perform acts altogether beyond their power. But we do insist that, in the light of God's method of dealing with the vast majority of men in the past, withholding the gospel effectually blunts its point. Ministers err grievously if they allow their hands to be tied or their mouths muzzled, thus disobeying Christ. The only difference between those living under the gospel and those who have only the light of nature seems to be that the grace of the one allotment is far greater than that of the other, that the responsibility is higher in proportion, and that the condemnation which results from disobedience must therefore be more severe in the one case than in the other in the great day of accounts. To those divinely called to preach the gospel the course is clear. They are to go forth in obedience to their commission, appealing to "every creature," urging their hearers to be reconciled to God.

Speaking for himself, the writer (who for more than twenty years was active in oral ministry) never found any other consideration to deter him from sounding forth the universal call of the gospel. He knew there might well be some in his congregation who had sinned that sin for which there is no forgiveness (Matt. 12:31-32), others who had probably sinned away their day of grace, having quenched the Spirit (1 Thess. 5:19) till it was no longer possible to renew them again to repentance (Luke 13:24-25; 19:48). Yet since this was mercifully concealed from him, he sought to cry aloud and spare not. He knew that the gospel was to be the savior of death unto death to some, and that God sometimes sends His servants forth with a commission similar to that of Isaiah's (6:9-10). Still that furnished no more reason why he should be silent than that the sun and moon should cease proclaiming their Creator's glory merely because the world is blind and deaf.

In this same connection it is pertinent to consider the striking and solemn case of Pharaoh. It indeed presents an awe—inspiring spectacle, yet that must not hinder us from looking at it and ascertaining what light it throws on the character and ways of the Most High. It is the case not merely of an isolated individual, but of a fearfully numerous class—the vessels of wrath fitted to destruction. It is true that Pharaoh was not called on to believe and be saved, he was not exhorted to yield himself to the constraining love of God as manifested in the gift of His Son; but he was required to submit himself to the authority of God and to accede to His revealed will. He was ordered to let Jehovah's people go that they might serve Him in the wilderness, and he was required to comply with the divine command not sullenly or reluctantly, not as a matter of necessity, but with his whole heart.

A Promise for Every Command of God

Let it not be overlooked that every divine command virtually implies a promise, for our duty and our welfare are in every instance inseparably joined (Deut. 10:12-13). If God is truly obeyed He will be truly glorified, and if He is truly glorified He will be truly enjoyed. Had the king of Egypt obeyed, certainly his fate would have been different. He would have been regarded not with disapproval but with favor; he would have been the object not of punishment but rather of reward. Nevertheless, it was not intended that he should obey. The Most High had decreed otherwise. Before Moses entered the presence of Pharaoh and made known Jehovah's command, the Lord informed His servant, "I will harden his heart that he shall not let the people go" (Ex. 4:21). This is unspeakably awful, yet it need not surprise us. The same sun whose rays melt the wax hardens the clay—an example in the visible realm of what takes place in the hearts of the renewed and of the unregenerate.

Not only was it God's intention to harden Pharaoh's heart so that he should not obey His command, but He plainly declared, "In very deed for this cause have I raised thee up; for to show in thee my power; and that my name may be declared throughout all the earth" (Ex. 9:16). The connection in which that solemn verse is quoted in Romans 9:17 makes it unmistakably plain that God ordained that this haughty monarch should be an everlasting monument to His severity. Here we witness the Ruler of this world dealing with men—for Pharaoh was representative of a large class—dealing with them about what concerns their highest interests, their happiness or their woe throughout eternity, not intending their happiness, not determining to confer the grace which would enable them to comply with His will, yet issuing commands to them, denouncing their threatenings, working signs and wonders before them, enduring them with much long-suffering while they add sin to sin and ripen for destruction. Yet let it be remembered that there was nothing which hindered Pharaoh from obeying except his own depravity. Whatever objection may be brought against the Word calling on the non-elect to repent and believe may with equal propriety be brought against the whole procedure of God with Pharaoh.

In their Articles of Faith the hyper-Calvinists declare, "We deny duty-faith and duty-repentance—these terms signifying that it is every man's duty to spiritually and savingly repent and believe." Those who belong to this school of theology insist that it would be just as sensible to visit our cemeteries and call on the occupants of the graves to come forth as to exhort those who are dead in trespasses and sins to throw down the weapons of their warfare and be reconciled to God. Such reasoning is unsound, for there is a vast and vital difference between a spiritually dead soul and a lifeless body. The soul of Adam became the subject of penal and spiritual death; nevertheless it retained all its natural powers. Adam did not lose all knowledge nor become incapable of volition; nor did the operations of conscience cease within him. He was still a rational being, a moral agent, a responsible creature, though he could no longer think or will, love or hate, in conformity to the law of righteousness.

It is far otherwise with physical dissolution. When the body dies it becomes as inactive, unintelligent and unfeeling as a piece of unorganized matter. A lifeless body has no responsibility, but a spiritually dead soul is accountable to God. A corpse in the cemetery will not "despise and reject" Christ (Isa. 53:3), will not "resist the Holy Ghost" (Acts 7:51), will not disobey the gospel (2 Thess. 1:8); but the sinner can and does do these very things, and is justly condemned for them. Are we, then, suggesting that fallen man is not "dead in trespasses and sins"? No indeed, but we do insist that those solemn words be rightly interpreted and that no false conclusions be drawn from them. Because the soul has been deranged by sin, because all its operations are unholy, it is correctly said to be in a state of spiritual death, for it no more fulfills the purpose of its being than does a dead body.

The fall of man, with its resultant spiritual death, did not dissolve our relation to God as the Creator, nor did it exempt us from His authority. But it forfeited His favor and suspended that communion with Him by which alone could be preserved that moral excellence with which the soul was originally endowed. Instead of attempting to draw analogies between spiritual and physical death and deriving inferences from them, we must stick very closely to the Scriptures and regulate all our thoughts by them. God's Word says, "You hath he quickened, who were dead in trespasses and sins: wherein in times past ye walked" (Eph. 2:1-2). Thus the spiritual death of the sinner is a state of active opposition against God—a state for which he is responsible, the guilt and enormity of which the preacher should constantly press upon him. Why do we speak of active opposition against God as being dead in sins? Because in Scripture "death" does not mean cessation of being, but a condition of separation and alienation from God (Eph. 4:18).

The solemn and humbling fact that fallen man is fully incapable of anything spiritually good or of turning to God is clearly revealed and insisted on in His Word (John 6:44; 2 Cor. 3:5, etc.), yet the majority of professing Christians have rejected that fact. It is important to note that the grounds and reasons for which it has been opposed by some are not scriptural. They do not allege that there is any specific statement of Holy Writ which directly contradicts it. They do not affirm that any passage can be produced from the Word which expressly tells us that fallen man has the power of will to do anything spiritually good, or that he is able by his own strength to turn to God, or even prepare himself to do so. Instead, they are obliged to fall back on a process of reasoning, making inferences and deductions from certain general principles which the Scriptures sanction. It is at once apparent that there is a vast difference in point of certainty between these two things.

Principle of Exhortation in Scripture

The principal objection made against the doctrine of fallen man's inability is drawn from the supposed inconsistency between it and the principle of exhortation which runs all through Scripture. It is pointed out that commands and exhortations are addressed to the descendants of Adam, that they are manifestly responsible to comply with them, that they incur guilt by failure to obey. Then the conclusion is drawn that, therefore, these commandments would never have been given, that such responsibility could not belong to man, and such guilt could not be incurred, unless they were able to will and to do the things commanded. Thus their whole argument rests not on anything actually stated in Scripture, but on certain notions respecting the reasons why God issued these commands and exhortations, and respecting the ground upon which moral responsibility rests.

In like manner we find the hyper-Calvinists pursuing an identical course in their rejection of the exhortation principle. Though at the opposite pole in doctrine—for they contend for the spiritual impotence of fallen man—yet they concur with others in resorting to a process of reasoning. They cannot produce a single passage from God's Word which declares that the unregenerate must not be urged to perform spiritual duties. They cannot point to any occasion on which the Savior Himself warned His apostles against such a procedure, not even when He commissioned them to go and preach His gospel. They cannot even discover a word from Paul cautioning either Timothy or Titus to be extremely careful when addressing the unsaved lest they leave their hearers with the impression that their case was far from being desperate.

Not only are the hyper-Calvinists unable to produce one verse of Scripture containing such prohibitions or warnings as we have mentioned above, but they are faced with scores of passages both in the Old and the New Testaments which show unmistakably that the servants of God in biblical times followed the very opposite course to that advocated by these twentieth century theorists. Neither the prophets, the Savior, nor His apostles shaped their policy by the state of their hearers. They did not accommodate their message according to the spiritual impotence of sinners, but plainly enforced the just requirements of a holy God. How, then, do these men dispose of all those passages which speak directly against their theories? By what is called (in some law courts) a process of "special pleading." We quote again from their Articles of Faith:

We believe that it would be unsafe, from the brief records we have of the way in which the apostles, under the immediate direction of the Lord, addressed their hearers in certain special cases and circumstances, to derive absolute and universal rules for ministerial addresses in the present day under widely-different circumstances.

Thus they naively attempt to neutralize and set aside the practice of our Lord and of His apostles. It is very much like the course followed by the Pharisees, who drew up their own rules and regulations, binding them upon the people, against whom Christ preferred the solemn charge of "making the word of God of none effect through your tradition" (Mark 7:13). The statement "We believe it would be unsafe" is lighter than chaff when weighed against the authority of Holy Writ. If God's servants today are not to be regulated by the recorded examples of their Master and His apostles, where shall they turn for guidance?

And why do the framers of these Articles of Faith consider it "unsafe" to follow the precedents furnished by the Gospels and the Acts? Their next Article supplies the answer:

Therefore, that for ministers in the present day to address unconverted persons, or indiscriminately all in a mixed congregation, calling upon them to savingly repent, believe, and receive Christ, or perform any other acts dependent upon the new-creative power of the Holy Ghost, is, on the one hand, to imply creature power, and, on the other, to deny the doctrine of special redemption.

Here they come out into the open and show their true colors, as mere rationalizers. They object to indiscriminate exhortations because they cannot see the consistency of such a policy with other doctrines. Just as extreme Arminians reject the truth of fallen man's moral impotence because they are unable to reconcile it with the exhortation principle, so Antinomians throw overboard human responsibility because they consider it out of harmony with the spiritual helplessness of the sinner.

Witness the consistency of man. As God Himself tells us, "Verily, every man at his best estate is altogether vanity" (Ps. 39:5). No wonder, then, that He bids us "Cease ye from man, whose breath is in his nostrils: for wherein is he to be accounted of?" (Isa. 2:22). Yes, "Cease ye from man"—religious man as much as irreligious man; cease placing any confidence in or dependence on him, especially in connection with spiritual and divine matters, for we cannot afford to be misdirected in these. Then what should the bewildered reader do? He must weigh everything he hears or reads in the balances of the Lord, testing it diligently by Holy Writ: "Prove all things; hold fast that which is good" (1 Thess. 5:21). And what is the servant of Christ to do? He must execute the commission his Master has given him, declare all the counsel of God (not mangled bits of it), and leave the Lord to harmonize what may seem contradictory to him—just as Abraham proceeded to obediently sacrifice Isaac, even though he was quite incapable of harmonizing God's command with His promise "In Isaac shall thy seed be called" (Gen. 21:12).

It will be no surprise to most of our readers that those ministers who are restricted from calling on the unsaved to repent and believe the gospel are also very slack in exhorting professing Christians. The divine commandments are almost entirely absent from their ministry. They preach a lot on doctrine, often on experience, but life conduct receives the scantiest notice. It is not too much to say that they seem to be afraid of the very word "duty." They preach soundly and beneficially on the obedience which Christ gave to God on behalf of His people, but they say next to nothing of that obedience which the Lord requires from those He has redeemed. They give many comforting addresses from God's promises, but they are woefully remiss in delivering searching messages on His precepts. If anyone thinks this charge is unfair, let him pick up a volume of sermons by any of these men and see if he can find a single sermon on one of the precepts.

As an example of what we have just mentioned we quote at some length from a series of "Meditations on the Preceptive part of the Word of God" by J. C. Philpot. Note that these were not the casual and careless utterances of the pulpit, but the deliberate and studied products of his pen. In his first article on the precepts of the Word of God, Mr. Philpot said:

It is a branch of Divine revelation which, without wishing to speak harshly or censoriously, has in our judgment been sadly perverted by many on the one hand, and we must say almost as sadly neglected, if not altogether ignored and passed by, by many on the other. . . . It is almost become a tradition in some churches professing the doctrines of grace to disregard the precepts and pass them by in a kind of general silence.

This declaration was sadly true, for the charge preferred characterized the greater part of his own ministry and applied to the preachers in his own denomination. That Mr. Philpot was fully aware of this sad state of affairs is clear from the following:

Consider this point, ye ministers, who Lord's day after Lord's day preach nothing but doctrine, doctrine, doctrine; and ask yourselves whether the same Holy Spirit who revealed the first three chapters of the epistle to the Ephesians did not also reveal the last three? Is not the whole epistle equally inspired, a part of that Scripture of which we read, "All Scripture is given by inspiration of God and is profitable for doctrine, for reproof, for correction, for instruction in righteousness, that the man of God may be perfect, thoroughly furnished unto all good works" (2 Tim. 3:16, 17)? How, then, can you be "a man of God perfect" (that is, complete as a minister) and "thoroughly furnished unto all good works," if you willfully neglect any part of that Scripture which God has given to be profitable to you, and to others by you? . . . Can it be right, can it be safe, can it be Scriptural, to treat all this fullness and weight of precept with no more attention than an obsolete Act of Parliament?

To the same effect, he declared:

To despise, then, the precept, to call it legal and burdensome, is to despise not man, but God, who hath given unto us His Holy Spirit in the inspired Scriptures for our faith and obedience. . . . Nothing more detects hypocrites, purges out loose professors, and fans away that chaff and dust which now so thickly covers our barn floors than an experimental handling of the precept. A dry doctrinal ministry disturbs no consciences. The loosest professors may sit under it, nay, be highly delighted with it, for it gives them a hope, if not a dead confidence, that salvation being wholly of grace they shall be saved whatever be their walk of life. But the experimental handling of the precept cuts down all this and exposes their hypocrisy and deception.

In developing his theme Mr. Philpot rightly began by discussing its importance, and this at considerable length. First, he called attention to its "bulk," or the large place given to precepts in the Word:

The amount of precept in the epistles, measured only by the test of quantity would surprise a person whose attention had not been directed to that point, if he would but carefully examine it. But it is sad to see how little the Scriptures are read amongst us with that intelligent attention, that careful and prayerful studiousness, that earnest desire to understand, believe, and experimentally realize their Divine meaning, which they demand and deserve, and which the Word of God compares to seeking as for silver, and searching "as for hid treasure" (Prov. 2:4).

How much less are the Scriptures read today than they were in Mr.

Philpot's time!

Next, he pointed out the following:

Were there no precepts in the New Testament we should be without an inspired rule of life, without an authoritative guide for our walk and conduct before the Church and the world. . . . But mark what would be the consequence if the preceptive part of the New Testament were taken out of its pages as so much useless matter. It would be like going on board of a ship bound on a long and perilous voyage, and taking out of her just before she sailed, all her charts, her compass, her sextants, her sounding line, her chronometer; in a word, all the instruments of navigation needful for her safely crossing the sea, or even leaving her port.

He disposed of the quibble that if there were no precepts, the church would still have the Holy Ghost to guide her by saying, "If God has mercifully and graciously given us rules and directions whereby to walk, let us thankfully accept them, not question and cavil how far we could have done without them."

Under his third reason for showing the importance of the precepts are some weighty remarks from which we select the following:

Without a special revelation of the precepts in the word of truth we should not know what was the will of God as regards all spiritual and practical obedience, so, without it as our guide and rule, we should not be able to live to His glory. . . . Be it, then, observed, and ever borne in mind that, as the glory of God is the end of all our obedience, it must be an obedience according to His own prescribed rule and pattern. In this point lies all the distinction between the obedience of a Christian to the glory of God and the self-imposed obedience of a Pharisee to the glory of self. . . . Thus we see that if there were no precepts as our guiding rule, we could not live to the glory of God, or yield to Him an acceptable obedience; and for this simple reason, that we should not know how to do so. We might wish to do so; we might attempt to do so; but we should and must fail.

This section on the importance of the precepts was denied by pointing out: "On its fulfillment turns the main test of distinction between the believer and the unbeliever, between the manifested vessel of mercy and the vessel of wrath fitted to destruction." At the close of this division he said, "Take one more test from the Lord's own lips. Read the solemn conclusion of the Sermon on the Mount—that grand code of Christian precepts."

After quoting Matthew 7:24-27 Mr. Philpot asks:

What is the Lord's own test of distinction between the wise man who builds on the rock, and the foolish man who builds on the sand? The rock, of course, is Christ, as the sand is self. But the test, the mark, the evidence, the proof of the two builders and the two buildings is the hearing of Christ's sayings and doing them, or the hearing of Christ's sayings and doing them not. We may twist and wriggle under such a text, and try all manner of explanations to parry off its keen, cutting edge; we may fly to arguments and deductions drawn from the doctrine of grace to shelter ourselves from its heavy stroke, and seek to prove that the Lord was there preaching the law and not the gospel, and that as we are saved by Christ's blood and righteousness, and not by our own obedience or our good works, either before or after calling, all such tests and all such texts are inapplicable to our state as believers. But after all our questionings and cavillings, our nice and subtle arguments, to quiet conscience and patch up a false peace, there the word of the Lord stands.

It is disastrous that such cogent arguments have carried little weight and that the precepts are still sadly neglected by many of the Lord's servants.

Chapter 7
Complement

Let us begin by defining our term. The "complement" of a thing is that which gives it completeness. In contemplating the natural condition of Adam's children we obtain a one-sided and misleading view if we confine our attention to their spiritual helplessness. That they are morally impotent, that they are totally depraved, that they are thoroughly under the bondage of sin, has been amply demonstrated. But that does not supply us with a complete diagnosis of their present state before God. Though fallen man is a wrecked and ruined creature, nevertheless he is still accountable to his Maker and Ruler. Though sin has darkened his understanding and blinded his judgment, he is still a rational being. Though his very nature is corrupt at its root, this does not exempt him from loving God with all his heart. Though he is "without strength," yet he is not "without excuse." And why not? Because side by side with fallen man's inability is his moral responsibility.

Moral Responsibility of Man

It is at this very point that the people of God, and especially His ministers, need to be much on their guard. If they appropriate one of the essential parts of the doctrine of Scripture but fail to lay hold of the equally essential supplementary part, then they will necessarily obtain a distorted view of the doctrine. "The word of God is quick, and powerful, and sharper than any two-edged sword" (Heb. 4:12). The word emphasized in the above quotation is of paramount importance, though its significance seems to be discerned by few today. Truth is twofold. Every aspect of truth presented in the Word is balanced by a counterpart aspect; every element of doctrine has its corresponding obligation. These two sides of the truth do not cross each other, but run parallel. They are not contradictory but complementary. The one aspect is just as essential as the other, and both must be retained if we are to be preserved from dangerous error. It is only as we hold firmly to "all the counsel of God" that we are delivered from the fatal pitfalls of false theology.

God Himself has illustrated this duality of truth by communicating the same concept to us in the form of the two Testaments, the Old and the New, the contents of which, broadly speaking, exemplify those two summaries of His nature and character: "God is light" (1 John 1:5); "God is love" (1 John 4:8). This same fundamental feature is seen again in the two principal communications which God has made, namely, His law and His gospel. That which characterizes the divine revelation in its broad outlines also holds equally good in connection with its details. Promises are balanced by precepts, the gifts of grace with the requirements of righteousness, the bestowments of abounding mercy with the exactions of inflexible justice. Correspondingly, the duties placed upon us answer to this twofold revelation of the divine character and will; as light and the Giver of the law, God requires the sinner to repent and the saint to fear Him; as love and the Giver of the gospel, the one is called upon to believe and the other to rejoice.

The doctrine of man's accountability and responsibility to God is set forth so plainly, so fully and so constantly throughout the Scriptures that he who runs may read it, and only those who deliberately close their eyes to it can fail to perceive its verity and force. The entire volume of God's Word testifies to the fact that He requires from man right affections and right actions, and that He judges and treats him according to these. "So then every one of us shall give account of himself to God" (Rom. 14:12) that the rights of God may be enforced upon moral agents. In the day of the revelation of His righteous judgment, God "will render to every man according to his deeds" (Rom. 2:5-6). Then will be fulfilled that word of Christ's "He that rejecteth me, and receiveth not my words, hath one that judgeth him: the word that I have spoken, the same shall judge him in the last day" (John 12:48). Men are responsible to employ in God's service the faculties He has given them (Matt. 25:14-30; Luke 12:48). They are responsible to improve the opportunities God has afforded them (Matt. 11:20-24; Luke 19:41-42).

Thus it is clear that—in keeping with the Word of God as a whole and with all His ways both in creation and providence—the doctrine of man's inability has a complementary and balancing doctrine, namely, his responsibility; and it is only by maintaining both in their due proportions that we shall be preserved from distorting the truth. But man is a creature of extremes, and his tendency to lopsidedness is tragically evidenced all through Christendom. The religious world is divided into opposing parties which contend for bits of the truth and reject others. Where can be found a denomination which preserves a due balance in its proclamation of God's law and God's gospel? In the presentation of God as light and God as love? In an equal emphasis on His precepts and His promises? And where shall we find a group of churches, or even a single church, which is preserving a due proportion in its preaching on man's inability and man's responsibility?

On every side today men in the pulpits pit one part of the truth against another, overstressing one doctrine and omitting its complement, setting those things against each other which God has joined together, confounding what He has separated. So important is it that God's servants should preserve the balance of truth, so disastrous are the consequences of a one-sided ministry, that we feel impressed to point out some of the more essential balancing doctrines which must be preserved if God is to be duly honored and His people rightly edified. We shall later resume the subject of human responsibility in order to throw light on the problem raised by the doctrine of man's impotence.

Means of Salvation

First, let us consider the causes and the means of salvation. There are no less than seven things which do concur in this great work, for all of them are said, in one passage or another, to "save" us. Salvation is ascribed to the love of God, to the atonement of Christ, to the mighty operations of the Spirit, to the instrumentality of the Word, to the labors of the preacher, to the conversion of a sinner, to the ordinances, or sacraments. The view of salvation entertained today by the majority of professing Christians is so superficial, so cramped, so inadequate. Indeed, so great is the ignorance which now prevails that we had better furnish proof texts for each of these seven concurring causes lest we be charged with error on so vital a subject.

Salvation is ascribed to God the Father "Who hath saved us, and called us with an holy calling" (2 Tim. 1:9)—because of His electing love in Christ. To the Lord Jesus: "He shall save his people from their sins" (Matt. 1:21)— because of His merits and satisfaction. To the Holy Spirit: "He hath saved us, by the renewing of the Holy Spirit" (Titus 3:5)—because of His almighty efficacy and operations. To the instrumentality of the Word, "the engrafted word, which is able to save your souls" (Jam. 1:21) —because it discovers to us the grace whereby we may be saved. To the labors of the preacher: "In doing this thou shalt both save thyself, and them that hear thee" (1 Tim. 4:16)—because of their subordination to God's work. To the conversion of a sinner in which repentance and faith are exercised by us: "Save yourselves from this untoward generation"—by the repentance spoken of in verse 38 (Acts 2:40); "By grace are ye saved through faith" (Eph. 2:8). To the ordinances, or sacraments: "Baptism doth also now save us" (1 Peter 3:21)— because it seals the grace of God to the believing heart.

Now these seven things must be considered in their order and kept in their place, otherwise incalculable harm will be done. For instance, if we elevate a subsidiary cause above a primary one, all sense of real proportion is lost. The love and wisdom of God comprise the prime cause, the first mover of all the rest of the causes which contribute to our salvation. Next are the merit and satisfaction of Christ, which are the result of the eternal wisdom and love of God and also the foundation of all that follows. The omnipotent operations of the Holy Spirit work in the elect those things which are necessary for their participation in and application of the benefits purposed by God and purchased by Christ. The Word is the chief means employed in conversion, for faith comes by hearing (Rom. 10:17). As the result of the Spirit's operations and His application of the Word, we are brought to repent and believe. In this it is the Spirit's general custom to employ the ministers of Christ as His subordinate agents. Baptism and the Lord's Supper are to confirm repentance and faith in us.

Not only must these seven concurring causes of salvation be considered in their proper order and kept in their due place, but they must not be confounded with one another so that we attribute to a later one what belongs to a primary one. We must not attribute to the ordinances that which belongs to the Word; the Word is appointed for conversion, the ordinances for confirmation. A legal contract is first offered and then sealed (ratified) when the parties are agreed: "Then they that [1] gladly received his word were [2] baptized" (Acts 2:41). Nor must we ascribe to the ordinances that which belongs to conversion. Many depend on their outward hearing of the Word as ground for partaking of the Lord's Supper: "We have eaten and drunk in thy presence, and thou hast taught in our streets" (Luke 13:26). But sound conversion, not frequenting the means of grace, is our title to pardon and life: "Be ye doers of the word, and not hearers only" (Jam. 1:22).

Again, we must not ascribe to conversion what belongs to the Spirit. Our repentance and faith are indispensable for the enjoyment of the privileges of Christianity, yet these graces do not spring from mere nature but are wrought in us by the Holy Spirit. Nor must we ascribe to the Spirit that honor which belongs to Christ, as if our conversion were meritorious, or that the repentance and faith worked in us deserved the benefits we have come to possess. No, that honor pertains to the Lamb alone, who merited and purchased all for us. Neither must we ascribe to Christ that which belongs to the Father, for the Mediator came not to take us away from God, but to bring us to Him: "Thou . . . hast redeemed us to God" (Rev. 5:9). Thus all things pertaining to our salvation must be ranged in their proper place, and we must consider what is peculiar to the love of God, the merit of Christ, the operations of the Spirit, the instrumentality of the Word, the labors of the preacher, the conversion of a sinner, the ordinances.

Unless we observe the true order of these causes and rightly predicate what pertains to each, we fall into disastrous mistakes and fatal errors. If we ascribe all to the mercy of God so as to shut out the merit of Christ, we exclude God's great design in the cross—to demonstrate His righteousness (Rom. 3:24-26). On the other hand, if we proclaim the atonement of Christ in a manner that lessens esteem of God's love, we are apt to form the false idea that He is all wrath and needed blood to appease Him; whereas Christ came to demonstrate His goodness (2 Cor. 5:19). If we ascribe to the merits of Christ that which is proper to the work of the Spirit, we confound things that are to be distinguished, as if Christ's blood could take us to heaven without a new nature being wrought in us. If we ascribe our conversion to the exercise of our own strength, we wrong the Holy Spirit. If, upon pretended conversion, we neglect the means and produce no good works, we err fatally.

Not only must these seven things not be confounded, but they must not be separated from one another. We cannot rest on the grace of God without the atonement and merits of Christ, for God does not exercise His mercy to the detriment of His justice. Nor can we rightly take comfort in the sacrifice of Christ without regeneration and true conversion wrought in us by the Spirit, for we must be vitally united to Christ before we can receive His benefits. Nor must we expect the operations of the Spirit without the instrumentality of the Word, for of the church it is said that Christ (by the Spirit) would "sanctify and cleanse it with the washing of water by the word" (Eph. 5:26). Nor must we conclude that we are regenerated by the Spirit without repentance and faith, for these graces are evidences of the new birth. Nor must the ordinances of baptism and the Lord's Supper be slighted; otherwise we dislocate the method by which God dispenses His grace.

Second, Christ must not be divided, either in His natures or His offices. There may be an abuse of the orthodox assertion of His deity, for if we reflect exclusively on that and neglect His great condescension in becoming flesh, we miss the chief intent of His incarnation—to bring God near to us in our nature. On the other hand, if we altogether consider Christ's humanity and overlook His Godhead, we are in danger of denying His super-eminent dignity, power and merit. Man is always disturbing the harmony of the gospel and setting one part against another. Unitarians deny that Christ is God and so impeach His atonement, pressing only His doctrine and example. Carnal men reflect only on Christ's redemption as the means of our atonement with God, and so overlook the necessary doctrine of His example, of Christ's appearing in order to be a pattern of obedience in our nature—so often pressed in Scripture (John 13:15; 1 Pet. 2:21; 1 John 2:6). Let us not put asunder what God has joined together.

So with Christ's offices. His general office is but one, to be Mediator, or Redeemer, but the functions which belong to it are three: prophetic, priestly and royal, one of which concerns His mediation with God, the other His dealings with us. We are to reflect on Him in both parts: "Consider the Apostle and High Priest of our profession, Christ Jesus" (Heb. 3:1). The work of an apostle has to do with men, that of a high priest with God. But some are so occupied with Christ's mediation with God that they give little thought to His dealings with men; others so consider His relation to men that they overlook His mediation with God. Regarding His very priesthood, some are so concerned with His sacrifice that they ignore His continual intercession and thus fail to appreciate what a comfort it is to present our requests by such a worthy hand to God; yet both are acts of the same office.

Great harm has been done by so preaching the sacrifice and intercession of Christ that His doctrine and government have been made light of. This is one of the most serious defects today in a considerable section of Christendom which prides itself on its orthodoxy. They look so much to the Savior that they have scarcely any eyes for the Teacher and Master. The whole religion of many professing Christians consists in depending on Christ's merits and trusting in His blood, without any real concern for His laws, by believing and obeying of which we are interested in the fruits of His righteousness and sacrifice. But the Word of God sets before us an entirely different sort of religion and does not make one office of the Redeemer disturb another. None find true rest for their souls until they take Christ's yoke upon them. He is the Savior of none unless He is first their Lord.

The Scriptures of truth set forth Christ under such terms as not only intimate privilege to us, but speak of duty and obedience as well. "God hath made that same Jesus . . . both Lord and Christ" (Acts 2:36). He is Lord, or supreme Governor, as well as Christ the anointed Savior; not only a Savior to redeem and bless, but a Lord to rule and command. "Him hath God exalted . . . to be a Prince and a Savior, for to give repentance to Israel, and forgiveness of sins" (Acts 5:31). Here again the compound terms occur because of His double work—to require and to give. Christ is such a Prince that He is also a Savior, and such a Savior that He is also a Prince; and as such He must be apprehended by our souls. Woe be to those who divide what God has joined. Also, "Christ is the head of the church: and he is the Savior of the body" (Eph. 5:23). On the one side, as Christ saves His people from their sins, so He also governs them; on the other side, His dominion over the church is exercised in bringing about its salvation.

The carnal segment of the religious world snatches greedily at comforts but has no heart for duties; it is all for privileges but wants nothing of obligations. This libertine spirit is very natural to all of us: "Let us break their bands asunder, and cast away their cords from us" (Ps. 2:3). It was thus with men when Christ was in their midst: "We will not have this man to reign over us" (Luke 19:14). Had He presented Himself to them simply as Redeemer He would have been welcome, but they had no desire for a Sovereign over them. Christ is wanted for His benefits, such as pardon, eternal life and everlasting glory; but the unregenerate cannot endure His strict doctrine and righteous laws—submission to His scepter is foreign to their nature.

On the other hand there are some who so extol the mediation of Christ with men that they ignore His mediation with God. Some are so absorbed with the letter of His doctrine that they overlook the necessity of the Holy Spirit to interpret it for them and apply it to their hearts. Men are such extremists that they cannot magnify one thing without deprecating another. They rejoice in the Spirit's communicating the Scriptures, but they deprecate His equally important work of opening hearts to receive them (Acts 16:14). Others so urge Christ as Lawgiver that they neglect Him as the fountain of grace. They are all for His doctrine and example, but despise His atonement and continued intercession. It is this taking of the gospel piecemeal instead of whole which has wrought such damage and corrupted the truth. Oh, for heavenly wisdom and grace to preserve the balance and to preach a full gospel.

We have pointed out that side by side with the fact of fallen man's spiritual impotence must be considered the complementary truth of his moral responsibility. We have sought to show the vital importance of holding fast to both and presenting them in their due proportions, thereby preserving the balance between them. In order to make this the more obvious and impressive, and at the same time to demonstrate the disastrous consequences of failing to do this, we have enlarged on the general principle of maintaining the gospel in its fullness instead of taking it piecemeal. We have endeavored to enforce the necessity for adhering to what God has joined together and of not confounding what He has separated, illustrating the point by a presentation of the seven concurring causes of salvation and of the natures and offices of Christ. We now resume that line of thought.

Third, the order of the covenant must not be disturbed. Said David of the Lord, "He hath made with me an everlasting covenant, ordered in all things, and sure" (2 Sam. 23:5). Certain writers have expressed themselves quite freely on the everlastingness of this covenant, and also on its sureness; but they have said very little on the ordering of it, and still less on the necessity of our abiding by its arrangements. No one will have any part in this covenant unless he is prepared to take the whole compact. Within the contract God has so arranged things that they may not and do not hinder one another. This order of the covenant appears chiefly in the right statement of privileges and conditions, means and ends, duties and comforts.

1. Privileges and conditions. "Through this man is preached unto you the forgiveness of sins: and by him all that believe are justified from all things" (Acts 13:38-39). Do not those words state a condition which excludes the infidel and includes the penitent believer? "If I wash thee not, thou hast no part with me," declared the holy Savior (John 13:8). Unless we are cleansed by Him we can have no part with Him in His benefits. "He became the author of the eternal salvation unto all them that obey him" (Heb. 5:9). Christ would act contrary to His divine commission, contrary to the covenant agreed upon by Him, were He to dispense His grace upon any other terms. Some men trust in their own external and imperfect righteousness, as if that were the only plea to make before God; whereas others look at nothing in themselves—either as conditions, evidence or means-and think their only plea is Christ's merits.

But neither those who trust in their own works nor those who think that no consideration is to be had for repentance, faith and new obedience adhere to the covenant of grace. Those who preach such a course offer men a covenant of their own modeling, not the covenant of God which is the sole charter and sure ground of the Christian's hope. The blood of Christ accomplishes its work, but repentance and faith must also do theirs. True, they have not the least degree of that honor which belongs to the love of God, the sacrifice of Christ or the operations of the Spirit; nevertheless repentance, faith and new obedience must be kept in view in their place. Is it not self-evident that none of the privileges of the covenant belong to the impenitent and unbelieving? It is the Father's work to love us, Christ's to redeem, and the Spirit's to regenerate; but we must accept the grace offered—that is, repent, believe and live in obedience to God.

2. Means and ends. There is a right order of means and ends, that by the former we may come to the latter. The greater end of Christianity is our coming to God, and the prime and general means are the office and work of Christ: "For Christ hath also once suffered for sins, the just for the unjust, that he might bring us to God" (1 Pet. 3:18). The subordinate means are the fruits of Christ's grace in sanctifying us and enabling us to overcome temptations—more expressly by patient suffering and active obedience. By patient suffering: "If so be that we suffer with him, that we may be also glorified together" (Rom. 8:17). "Wherefore let them that suffer according to the will of God commit the keeping of their souls to him in well doing, as unto a faithful Creator" (1 Pet. 4:19). By obedience: "Know ye not, that to whom ye yield yourselves servants to obey, his servants ye are to whom ye obey; whether of sin unto death, or of obedience unto righteousness?" (Rom. 6:16). "He that saith, I know him, and keepeth not his commandments, is a liar, and the truth is not in him" (1 John 2:4).

Now the great difficulty in connection with our salvation (1 Pet. 4:18) lies not in a respect to the end but the means. There is some difficulty about the end, namely, to convince men of an unseen bliss and glory; but there is far more about the means. There is not only greater difficulty in convincing their minds, but in gaining their hearts and bringing them to submit to that patient, holy, self-denying course whereby they may obtain eternal life. Men wish the end, but refuse the means. Like Balaam (Num. 23:10) they want to die the death of the righteous, but are unwilling to live the life of the righteous. When the Israelites despised the land of Canaan (Ps. 106:24-25) it was because of the difficulty of getting to it. They were assured that Canaan was a land flowing with milk and honey, but when they learned there were giants to be overcome first, walled towns to be scaled and numerous inhabitants to be vanquished, they demurred. Heaven is a glorious place, but it can only be reached by the way of denying self; and this few are willing to do. But the covenant expressly urges this upon us (Matt. 16:24; Luke 14:26).

3. Duties and comforts. Also there is a right order of duties and comforts. "Come unto me, all ye that labour and are heavy laden, and I will give you rest. Take my yoke upon you, and learn of me; for I am meek and lowly in heart: and ye shall find rest unto your souls" (Matt. 11:28-29). Observe carefully how commands and comforts, precepts and promises are here interwoven, and let us not separate what God has joined together. We must diligently attend to both in our desires and practices alike. We must not pick and choose what suits us best and pass by the rest, but earnestly seek after God and diligently use all His appointed means

that He may "fulfill all the good pleasure of his goodness, and the work of faith with power" (2 Thess. 1:11). But of how many must God say, as He did of old, "Ephraim is as a heifer that is taught and loveth to tread out the corn, but will not break the clods" (Hosea 10:11, an ancient translation). People desire privileges but neglect duties; they are all for wages but reluctant to work for them.

So it is even in the performance of duties: some are welcomed and done, others are disliked and shirked. But every duty must be observed in its place and season, and one must never be set against another. In resisting sin some avoid sensuality but yield to worldliness, deny fleshly lusts but fall into deadly errors. So with graces: Christians look so much to one that they forget the others. We are told to take unto ourselves "the whole armor of God" (Eph. 6:11), not simply a breastplate without a helmet. We must not play up knowledge so as to neglect practice, nor fervor of devotion so as to mislead us into ignorance and blind superstition. Some set their whole hearts to mourn for sin and think little of striving after a sense of their Savior's love; others prattle of free grace but are not watchful against sin nor diligent in being fruitful.

Lest some imagine that we have departed from the landmarks of our fathers and have inculcated a spirit of legality, we propose to supply a number of quotations from the writings of some of the most eminent of God's servants in the past, men who in their day lifted up their voices in protest against the lopsided ministry which we are decrying, and who stressed the vital importance of preserving the balance of truth and of according to each segment its due place and emphasis. For the evil we are resisting is no new thing, but one that has wrought much havoc in every generation. The pendulum has ever swung from one extreme to the other, and few have been the men who preserved the happy mean or who faithfully declared all the counsel of God.

We begin with a portion of Bishop J. C. Ryle's Estimate of Manton, the Puritan:

Manton held strongly the need of preventing and calling grace; but that did not hinder him from inviting all men to repent, believe, and be saved. Manton held strongly that faith alone lays hold on Christ and appropriates justification; but that did not prevent him urging upon all the absolute necessity of repentance and turning from sin. Manton held strongly to the perseverance of God's elect; but that did not hinder him from teaching that holiness is the grand distinguishing mark of God's people, and that he who talks of "never perishing" while he continues in willful sin, is a hypocrite and a self-deceiver. In all this I frankly confess I see much to admire. I admire the Scriptural wisdom of a man who, in a day of hard and fast systems, could dare to be apparently inconsistent in order to "declare all the counsel of God." I firmly believe that this is the test of theology which does good in the church of Christ. The man who is not tied hand and foot by systems, and does not pretend to reconcile what our imperfect eyesight cannot reconcile in this dispensation, he is the man whom God will bless.

If Manton were on earth today we do not know where he would be able to obtain a hearing. One class would denounce him as a Calvinist, while another would shun him as an Arminian. One would accuse him of turning the grace of God into lasciviousness, while another would charge him with gross legality. All would say he was not consistent with himself, that one of his sermons contradicted another; that he was a "yea and nay preacher," one day building up and the next day tearing down what he had previously erected. So long as he confined himself to what their Articles of Faith expressed, Calvinists would allow him to address them; but as soon as he began to press duties upon them and exhort to performance of those duties, he would be banished from their pulpits. Arminians would tolerate him just so long as he kept to the human responsibility side of the truth, but the moment he mentioned unconditional election or particular redemption they would close their doors against him.

That prince of theologians, John Owen, in his work "The Causes, Ways, and Means of Understanding the Mind of God," after fully establishing "the necessity of an especial work of the Holy Spirit in the illumination of our minds to make us understand the mind of God as revealed in the Scriptures," and before treating of the means which must be used and the diligent labors put forth by us, began his fourth chapter by anticipating and disposing of an objection. A certain class of extremists (termed enthusiasts in those days) argued that, if our understanding of the Scriptures was dependent upon the illuminating operations of the Holy Spirit, then there was no need for earnest effort and laborious study on our part. After affirming that the gracious operations of the Spirit "do render all our use of proper means for the right interpretation of the Scripture, in a way of duty, indispensably necessary," Mr. Owen went on to point out:

But thus it hath fallen out in other things. Those who have declared anything either of doctrine or of the power of the grace of the Gospel, have been traduced as opposing the principles of morality and reason, whereas on their grounds alone, their true value can be discovered and their proper use directed. So the apostle preaching faith in Christ with righteousness and justification thereby, was accused to have made void the law, whereas without his doctrine the law would have been void, or of no use to the souls of men. So he pleads "Do we then make void the law through faith? God forbid: yea, we establish the law" (Rom. 3:31). So to this day, justification by the imputation of the righteousness of Christ and the necessity of our own obedience, the efficacy of Divine grace in conversion and the liberty of our wills, the stability of God's promises and our diligent use of means, are supposed inconsistent.

It will be seen from the closing sentences of the above quotation that there were some in the days of the Puritans who made a god of consistency, or rather of what they considered to be consistent, and that they pitted parts of the truth against their own favorite doctrines, rejecting anything which they considered to be inharmonious or incongruous. But Owen refused to accede to them and preferred to be regarded as inconsistent with himself rather than withhold those aspects of the gospel which he well knew were equally glorifying to God and profitable for His people. It is striking to note that the particular things singled out by him for mention are the very ones objected to by the hyper-Calvinists today, which shows how far astray they are from what Owen taught. We continue to quote from him:

So it is here also. The necessity of the communication of spiritual light unto our minds to enable us to understand the Scriptures, and the exercise of our own reason in the use of external means, are looked on as irreconcilable. But as the apostle saith, "Do we make void the law by faith? yea, we establish it;" though he did it not in that place, nor unto those ends that the Jews would have had and used it. So we may say, do we by asserting the righteousness of Christ make void our own obedience, by the efficacy of grace destroy the liberty of our wills, by the necessity of spiritual illumination take away the use of reason? yea, we establish them. We do it not, it may be, in such a way or in such a manner as some would fancy and which would render them all on our part really useless, but in a clear consistency with and proper subservience unto the work of God's Spirit and grace.

"The people answered him, We have heard out of the law that Christ abideth for ever: and how sayest thou, The Son of man must be lifted up?" (John 12:34). In his comments upon this verse, that grand old commentator Matthew Henry said:

They alleged those scriptures of the O.T. which speak of the perpetuity of the Messiah, that He should be so far from being cut off in the midst of His days, that He should be a "Priest forever" (Psa. 110:4) and a King "forever" (Psa. 89:29, etc.). That He should have length of days forever and ever, and His years "as many generations" (Psa. 61:6); from all this they inferred the Messiah should not die. Thus great knowledge in the letter of the Scripture, if the heart be unsanctified, is capable of being abused to serve the cause of infidelity and to fight Christianity with its own weapons. Their perverseness will appear if we consider that when they vouched the Scripture to prove that the Messiah "abideth forever," they took no notice of those texts which speak of the Messiah's death and sufferings: they had heard out of the law that He "abideth forever," but had they never heard out of the law that Messiah "shall be cut off" (Dan. 9:26), that He shall "pour out His soul unto death" (Isa. 53:12), and particularly that His "hands and feet" should be pierced? Why then do they make so strange of His being "lifted up?"

The folly of these skeptical Jews was not one whit greater than that of rationalistic Calvinists. The one group refused to believe one part of Messianic prophecy because they were unable to harmonize it with another; the latter reject the truth of human responsibility because they cannot perceive its consistency with the doctrine of fallen man's spiritual impotence. Aptly did Matthew Henry follow up the above remarks by immediately adding:

We often run into great mistakes, and then defend them with Scripture arguments, by putting those things asunder which God in His Word has put together, and opposing one truth under the pretence of supporting another. We have heard out of the Gospel that which exalts free grace, we have heard also that which enjoins duty, and we must cordially embrace both, and not separate them, or set them at variance.

Divine grace is not bestowed with the object of freeing men from their obligations but rather with that of supplying them with a powerful motive for more readily and gratefully discharging those obligations. To make God's favor a ground of exemption from the performance of duty comes perilously near to turning His grace into lasciviousness.

In his "Precious Remedies Against Satan's Devices," Thomas Brooks wrote:

The fourth device Satan hath to keep souls off from holy exercises, is by working them to make false inferences on those blessed and glorious things that Christ hath done. As that Jesus Christ hath done all for us, therefore there is nothing for us to do but to joy and rejoice. He hath perfectly justified us, fulfilled the law, satisfied Divine justice, pacified His Father's wrath, and is gone to Heaven to prepare a place for us, and in the meantime to intercede for us; and therefore away with praying, mourning, hearing, etc. Ah! what a world of professors hath Satan drawn in these days from religious services by working them to make such sad, wild and strange inferences from the excellent things the Lord Jesus hath done for His beloved ones.

The Puritan named one remedy for this:

To dwell as much on those scriptures that show you the duties and services that Christ requires of you, as upon those scriptures that declare to you the precious and glorious things Christ hath done for you. It is a sad and dangerous thing to have two eyes to behold our dignity and privileges, and not one to see our duties and services. I should look with one eye upon the choice things Christ hath done for me to raise up my heart to love Christ with the purest love and to joy in Him with the strongest joy, and to lift up Christ above all who hath made Himself to be my all; and I should look with the other eye upon those services and duties that the scriptures require of those for whom Christ hath done such blessed things, as 1 Cor. 6:19, 20; 15:58; Gal. 6:9; 1 Thess. 5:16, 17; Phil. 2:12; Heb. 10:24, 25. Now a soul that would not be drawn away by this device of Satan must not look with a squint eye upon these blessed scriptures, and many more of like import, but he must dwell upon them, make them to be his chiefest and choicest companions, and this will be a happy means to keep him close to Christ.

Our principal design in writing further on the fact that man's spiritual impotence is his moral responsibility is to make plainly manifest the tremendous importance of preserving the balance of truth, which is mainly a matter of setting forth each element of it in its scriptural proportions. Almost all theological and religious error consists of truth perverted, truth wrongly divided, truth misapplied, truth overemphasized, truth viewed in a wrong perspective. The fairest face on earth, possessed of the most comely features, would soon become ugly and unsightly if one feature continued growing while the others remained undeveloped. Physical beauty is mainly a thing of due proportion. And thus it is with the Word of God: Its beauty and blessedness are best perceived when it is presented in its true proportions. Here is where so many have failed in the past; some favorite doctrine has been concentrated on, and others of equal importance neglected.

Need for Balanced Teaching

It is freely granted that in these degenerate days the servant of God is often called upon to give special emphasis to those verities of Holy Writ which are now so generally ignored and denied. Yet even here much wisdom is needed lest our zeal run away with us. The requirements of that phrase meat in due season" must ever be borne in mind. When working among Arminians we should not altogether omit the human responsibility side of the truth, yet the main emphasis ought to be placed on the divine sovereignty and its corollaries, which are so sadly perverted, if not blankly denied, by free-willers. Contrariwise, when ministering to Calvinists our chief aim should be to bring before them not those things they most like to hear, but those which they most need—those aspects of truth they are least familiar with. Only thus can we be of the greatest service to either group.

To illustrate what we have just said, take the subject of prayer. In preaching on it to Arminians, it would be well to define very clearly what this holy exercise is not designed to accomplish and what is its spiritual aim, showing that our prayers are not intended for the overcoming of any reluctance in God to grant the mercies we need, still less our supplications meant to effect any change in the divine purpose. "The counsel of the Lord standeth forever, the thoughts of his heart to all generations" (Ps. 33:11). Rather the purpose of prayer is the subjecting of ourselves to God in asking for those things which are according to His will. In preaching to Calvinists we should warn against that fatalistic attitude which assumes that it will make no difference to the event whether we petition God or not, reminding them that "the effectual fervent prayer of a righteous man availeth much" (Jam.5:16). Some Arminians need rebuking for irreverence and unholy familiarity in addressing the Most High, while some Calvinists should be encouraged to approach the throne of grace with holy boldness, with the liberty of children petitioning their father.

The same course needs to be followed when expounding the great subject of salvation. Discrimination must be used as to which aspects most need to be set before any particular congregation. The manner in which this most blessed theme should be presented calls for much understanding, not only of the subject itself but also of the truth. Some doctrines are more difficult to apprehend than others (2 Peter 3:16), and they need to be approached gradually and given out "here a little, there a little." We are well aware that in offering such counsel we lay ourselves open to the charge of acting craftily; in reality we are simply advocating the very policy pursued by Christ and His apostles. Of the Savior it is recorded that "with many such parables spoke he the word unto them, as they were able to hear it" (Mark 4:33); and addressing His apostles He said, "I have yet many things to say unto you, but ye cannot bear them now" (John 16:12; cf. 1 Cor. 3:1-2; 9:19-22).

What we have advocated above is simply adopting our presentation of the truth according to the state of our congregation. There is a vast difference between presenting the way of salvation to the unconverted and expounding the doctrine of salvation to those who are converted, though too many preachers make little distinction here. Great care needs to be exercised when preaching from one of the Epistles to a general congregation, lest on the one hand the children's bread be cast to the dogs or, on the other, seekers after the Lord be stumbled. While it is true that, in the absolute sense, no sinner can save himself or even contribute anything toward his salvation by any physical or mental act of his own, yet he must be constantly reminded that the gospel sets before him an external Savior (rather than One who is working secretly and invincibly in him) whom he is responsible to promptly receive on the terms by which He is offered, to him.

It is most important that pulpit and pew alike should have a right conception of the relation of faith to salvation—a full-orbed conception and not a restricted and one-sided view. Believing is not only an evidence of salvation and a mark of regeneration, but it is also necessary in order to obtain salvation. True, the sinner is not saved for his faith; yet it is equally true that he cannot be saved without it. That believing is in one sense a saving act is clearly affirmed: "But we are not of them who draw back unto perdition; but of them that believe to the saving of the soul" (Heb. 10:39). Take the case of Cornelius. It is plain from Acts 10:2, 4 that a work of grace had been wrought in his heart before Peter was sent to him; yet Acts 11:14 makes it equally clear that it was necessary for the apostles to go and speak words "whereby he and his house should be saved." One of those "words" was "To him give all the prophets witness, that through his name whosoever believeth in him shall receive remission of sins" (10:43). Let it not be objected that we are hereby making a savior of faith, for Christ did not hesitate to say "Thy faith hath saved thee" (Luke 7:50).

As an example of how well Calvin himself preserved the balance of truth we quote the following from his Institutes:

Yet at the same time a pious man will not overlook inferior causes. Nor, because he accounts those from whom he has received any benefit, the ministers of the Divine goodness, will he therefore cast them by unnoticed, as though they deserved no thanks for their kindness; but will feel and readily acknowledge his obligation to them, and study to return it as ability and opportunity may permit. Finally, he will reverence and praise God as the principal Author of benefits received, will honor men as His ministers; and will understand, what, indeed, is the fact, that the will of God has laid him under obligations to those persons by whose means the Lord has been pleased to communicate His benefits.

While ascribing supreme honor and glory to the Author of every blessing, we must not despise the instruments He may design to employ in the imparting of them.

The great Reformer went on:

If He suffer any loss either through negligence or through imprudence, he will conclude that it happened according to the Divine will, but will also impute the blame of it to himself. If any one be removed by disease, whom, while it was his duty to take care of him, he has treated with neglect,—though he cannot be ignorant that that person had reached those limits which it was impossible for him to pass, yet he will not make this a plea to extenuate his guilt; but, because he has not faithfully performed his duty towards him, will consider him as having perished through his criminal negligence. Much less, when fraud and preconceived malice appear in the perpetration either of murder or of theft, will he excuse those enormities under the pretext of the Divine Providence: in the same crime he will distinctly contemplate the righteousness of God and the iniquity of man, as they respectively discover themselves.

How far was Calvin from the squint-eyed vision of many who claim to be his admirers! Writing on "the conducting of prayer in a right and proper manner," he stated:

The fourth and last rule is, That thus prostrate with true humility, we should nevertheless be animated to pray by the certain hope of obtaining our requests. It is indeed an apparent contradiction to connect a certain confidence of God's favor with a sense of His righteous vengeance, though these two things are perfectly consistent if persons oppressed by their own guilt be encouraged solely by the Divine goodness. For as we have before stated that repentance and faith, of which one terrifies and the other exhilarates, are inseparably connected, so their union is necessary in prayer. And this agreement is briefly expressed by David: "I will come into Thy house in the multitude of Thy mercy: and in Thy fear will I worship toward Thy holy temple" (Psa. 5:7). Under the goodness of God he comprehends faith, though not to the exclusion of fear, for His majesty not only commands our reverence, but our own unworthiness makes us forget all pride and security and fills us with fear. I do not mean a confidence which delivers the mind from all sense of anxiety, and soothes it into pleasant and perfect tranquility, for such a placid satisfaction belongs to those whose prosperity is equal to their wishes, who are affected by no care, corroded by no anxiety and alarmed by no fear. And the saints have an excellent stimulus to calling upon God when their needs and perplexities harass and disquiet them and they are almost despairing in themselves, till faith opportunity relieves them; because amid such troubles the goodness of God is so glorious in their view, that though they groan under the pressure of present calamities and are likewise tormented with the fear of greater in future, yet a reliance on it alleviates the difficulty of bearing them and encourages a hope of deliverance.

Here we have brought together two radically different exercises of the mind, which are totally diverse in their springs, their nature and their tendency—fear and confidence, perturbation and tranquility: two spiritual graces which some imagine neutralize each other—humility and assurance. A sight of God's ineffable holiness fills a renewed heart with awe; and when it is coupled with a sense of His high majesty and inflexible righteousness, the soul—conscious of its excuseless sins, its defilement and its guilt—is made to fear and tremble, feeling utterly unfit and unworthy to address the Most High. Yes, but if the humbled saint is able to also contemplate the goodness of God, view Him as the Father of mercies and consider some of His exceeding great and precious promises which are exactly suited to his dire needs, he is encouraged to hope. And while his humility does not then degenerate into presumption, yet is he constrained to come boldly to the throne of grace and present his petitions.

Calvin spoke clearly on this point:

The prayers of a pious man, therefore, must proceed from both these dispositions, and must also contain and discover them both: though he must groan under present evils and is anxiously afraid of new ones, yet at the same time he must resort for refuge to God, not doubting His readiness to extend the assistance of His hand. For God is highly displeased by our distrust, if we supplicate Him for blessings which we have no expectation of receiving. There is nothing, therefore, more suitable to the nature of prayers, than that they be conformed to this rule:—not to rush forward with temerity, but to follow the steps of faith. "If any of you lack wisdom, let him ask of God, that giveth to all men liberally, and upbraideth not. But let him ask in faith, nothing wavering" (Jam. 1:5, 6). Where, by opposing "faith" to "wavering" he very aptly expresses its nature. And equally worthy of attention is what he adds, that they avail nothing who call upon God in unbelief and doubt, and are uncertain in their minds whether they shall be heard or not.

The charge preferred by God against Israel's priests of old—"Ye have not kept my ways, but have been partial in the law" (Mal. 2:9)—applies to many preachers today. Some have gone to such extremes that they have denied there is any such thing as God chastising His own dear children. They argue that since "he hath not beheld iniquity in Jacob, neither hath he seen perverseness in Israel" (Num. 23:21), and since He has declared of His bride, "Thou art all fair, my love; there is no spot in thee" (Song of Sol. 4:7), there remains no occasion for the rod. It is this dwelling on favorite portions of truth to the exclusion of others which has led many into grievous errors. The non-imputation of sin to believers and the chastising of sin in believers are both plainly taught in the Scriptures (e.g., 2 Sam. 12:13-14 where both facts are mentioned side by side). Whether or not they can be reconciled to mere human reason, both must be firmly held by us.

As Matthew Henry tersely expressed it, "In the doctrine of Christ there are paradoxes which to men of corrupt mind are stumblingstones." It is the twofoldness of truth which has (in part) furnished occasion for infidels to declare that the Bible is full of contradictions; being blind spiritually, they are unable to perceive the perfect harmony of the whole. To what a sorry pass have things come, then, when some who wish to be regarded as the very champions of orthodoxy make the same charge against those who contend for the entire faith once delivered to the saints. The truth, the whole truth, and nothing but the truth, is the standard which must be applied to the pulpit as well as the lawcourt. One element of truth must not be pressed to such an extreme that another is denied; each must be given its due and distinctive place.

It is a favorite device of Satan's to drive us from one extreme to another. This may be seen by observing the order of the temptations which he set before the Savior. First he sought to overthrow Christ's faith, to bring Him to doubt the Word of God and His goodness to Him. He said something like this: "God has proclaimed from heaven that Thou art His beloved Son, yet He is allowing Thee to starve to death here in the wilderness," as is clear from his "If thou be the Son of God, command that these stones be made bread." Failing to prevail by such an assault, Satan then took a contrary course in his next attack, seeking to bring the Lord Jesus to act presumptuously: "If thou be the Son of God, cast thyself down: for it is written, He shall give his angels charge concerning thee: and in their hands they shall bear thee up, lest at any time thou dash thy foot against a stone." The force of this was: "Since Thou art so fully assured of the Father's loving care, demonstrate Thy confidence in His protection; since Thy faith in His Word is so unshakable, count upon His promise that no harm shall befall Thee even though Thou castest Thyself from the pinnacle of the temple."

The above has been recorded for our learning, for it shows us the guile of the devil and the cunning tactics which he employs, especially that of swinging from one extreme to another. Let it be borne in mind that as he dealt there with Christ the Head, so Satan continues to act with all Christ's members. If he cannot bring them to one extreme, he will endeavor to drive them to another. If he cannot bring a man to covetousness and miserliness, he will attempt to drive him to prodigality and thriftlessness. If a man is of the sober and somber type, let him beware lest the devil, in condemning him for this, lead him into levity and irreverence. The devil cannot endure one who turns neither to the right hand nor to the left; nevertheless, we must seek to keep the golden mean, neither doubting on the one hand nor presuming on the other, giving way neither to despair nor to recklessness.

Let us not forget that truth itself may be misused (2 Pet. 3:16), and the very grace of God may be turned into lasciviousness (Jude 4). Solemn warnings are these. "Commit thy way unto the Loan; trust also in him; and he shall bring it to pass" (Ps. 37:5). That is a blessed promise, yet I altogether pervert it if I use it to the neglect of duty and sit down and do nothing. "Stand fast therefore in the liberty wherewith Christ hath made us free" (Gal. 5:1). That is an important precept, yet I put it to wrong use if I so stand up for my own rights that I exercise no love for my brothers in Christ. "Who are kept by the power of God through faith unto salvation ready to be revealed in the last time" (1 Pet. 1:5). That too is a blessed promise, yet it does not exempt me from using all proper means for my preservation. The Christian farmer knows that unless God is pleased to bless his labors he will reap no harvest, but that does not hinder him from plowing and harrowing.

Let us close these remarks by a helpful quotation from one who showed the perfect consistency between Romans 8:38-39 and 1 Corinthians 9:27: "But I keep under my body, and bring it into subjection: lest that by any means, when I have preached to others, I myself should be a castaway."

Charles Hodge stated:

The reckless and listless Corinthians thought they could safely indulge themselves to the very verge of sin; while this devoted apostle considered himself as engaged in a life-struggle for his salvation. The same apostle, however, who evidently acted on the principle that the righteous scarcely are saved and that the kingdom of heaven suffereth violence, at other times breaks out in the most joyous assurance of salvation, and says that he was persuaded that nothing in heaven, earth or hell could ever separate him from the love of God. The one state of mind is the necessary condition of the other. It is only those who are conscious of this constant and deadly struggle with sin, to whom this assurance is given. In the very same breath Paul says, "O wretched man that I am" and "thanks be to God who giveth us the victory" (Rom. 7: 24, 25). It is the indolent and self-empty professor who is filled with a carnal confidence.

Chapter 8
Elucidation

Had we followed a strictly logical order, this branch of our subject would have immediately followed our discussion of the problem which is raised by this doctrine. But we considered it better to first build a broader foundation for our present remarks by considering its "complement." We showed (1) that there is a twofoldness of truth which characterizes the whole of divine revelation; (2) that parallel with the fact of man's spiritual impotence runs his full responsibility; (3) that the acid test of sound theology consists in preserving the balance of truth or presenting its component parts in their proper perspective; (4) that the servant of God must always strive to set forth each aspect of the gospel in its fair proportions, being impervious to the charge of inconsistency which is sure to be hurled at him by extremists.

God's Requirements Versus Man's Impotence
Let us now restate the problem to which this and the following chapters endeavor to present a solution. How can fallen man be held responsible to glorify God when he is incapable of doing so? How can it conform with the mercy of God for Him to require the debt of obedience when we are unable to pay it? How can it consist with the justice of God to punish with eternal suffering for the neglect of what lies altogether beyond the sinner's power? If fallen man be bound fast with the cords of sin, with what propriety can God demand of him the performance of a perfect holiness? Since the sinner is the slave of sin, how can he be a free agent? Can he really be held accountable for not doing what it is impossible for him to do? If the fall has not annulled human responsibility, must it not to a considerable extent have modified it?

It is not for the benefit of the carping critic or the objecting infidel that we take up such questions as these, but with the desire to help our fellow Christians. Though such problems do not to the least degree shake their confidence in the character of the Lord or the integrity of His Word, some believers are at a loss to see how His ways can be equal. On the one hand Scripture declares, "The carnal mind is enmity against God: for it is not subject to the law of God, neither indeed can be." Therefore it is incapable of doing anything else but sin: "So then they that are in the flesh cannot please God" (Rom. 8:7-8). Yet on the other we are informed that "the wrath of God is revealed from heaven against all ungodliness and unrighteousness of men" (Rom. 1:18) and that "every transgression and disobedience" shall receive "a just recompense of reward" (Heb. 2:2). Nor is any deliverance from God's wrath obtainable through the gospel except on such conditions as no natural man can comply with; nevertheless, noncompliance with those conditions brings additional condemnation.

To those who give serious thought to this subject it almost seems to make out the Most High to be what the slothful servant said: "Reaping where thou hast not sown, and gathering where thou hast not strewed" (Matt. 25:24). That this is far from being the case every regenerate heart is fully assured, yet the removal of this God-dishonoring suspicion is earnestly desired by those who are perplexed by it. These points have engaged our mind for many years, and it is our desire to pass on to other members of the household of faith what has been a help to us. How fallen man can be morally impotent yet morally responsible is the matter we shall try to elucidate.

In seeking the solution to our problem we shall first aim to cast upon it the light furnished by the relationship which exists between the Creator and the creature, between God and fallen man. When facing the difficulties raised by the truth of the moral impotence of fallen man, it is of vast importance that we clearly recognize and tenaciously hold the fact that God has not forfeited His right over the creature even though the creature has lost his power to meet God's requirements. At this point, especially, much of the difficulty is removed. Further light is thrown upon the nature of human responsibility when we obtain a right view of man's moral agency. By far the greater part of the difficulty vanishes when we correctly define and state the nature of man's impotence: what it is not, and what it does consist of. Finally, it will be found that man's own conscience and consciousness bear witness to the fact of his accountability.

In seeking to show the relationship which exists between the Creator and the creature, between God and the fallen man, let us inquire, What is the foundation of moral obligation? What is the rule of human duty? It should be evident to any anointed eye that there can be only one answer to these questions: The will of God, the will of God as revealed to us. God is our Maker and as such He has the right to unlimited control over the creatures of His hands. That right of God is absolute, uncontrolled and without any limitation. It is the right of the potter over the clay. Moreover, the creature is entirely dependent upon the Creator: "In him we live, and move, and have our being" (Acts 17:28). He that "formeth the spirit of man within him" sustains that spirit and the body which it inhabits. In reference to our bodies we have no self-sustaining power; let God's hand be withdrawn, and we return to the dust. The soul of man is equally dependent upon the sustaining power of God.

Man's Obligation

Because God is who He is and because man is the work of His hands, the will of God must be the foundation of moral obligation. "All things were created by him, and for him" (Col. 1:16). "Thou hast created all things, and for thy pleasure they are and were created" (Rev. 4:11). But God is not only our Creator. He is also our Ruler and Governor, and His rights over us are made known by His will, by His expressed will. Man is bound to do what God commands and to abstain from what He forbids, simply because He commands and forbids. Beyond that there is no reason. Direct reference to the divine will is essential to any moral virtue. When an action is done regardless of God's will, no honor is shown Him and no virtue pertains to it. Such is the clear and definite teaching of Holy Writ; it knows no foundation of right or wrong, no obligation, except the will of the Most High.

It therefore follows that the will of God revealed is the rule of duty. It is self-evident that the will of God cannot direct and govern us except as it is made known to us, and in His Word it is made known. God's own rule of action is His will, for there can be no higher or holier rule. "He doeth according to his will in the army of heaven, and among the inhabitants of the earth" (Dan. 4:35); "He saith to Moses, I will have mercy on whom I will have mercy, and I will have compassion on whom I will have compassion" (Rom. 9:15). To the will of God our blessed Redeemer uniformly referred as both the obligation and rule of His own action. "I delight to do thy will, o my God: yea, thy law is within my heart" (Ps. 40:8); "I seek not mine own will, but the will of the Father which hath sent me" (John 5:30). Even when the desire of His sinless humanity was for an escape from the awful cup, His holy soul felt the binding obligation of the divine will: "Not as I will, but as thou wilt." Does not that settle the question once for all? If the incarnate Son looked no higher, no lower, no farther, why should we? Compliance with the will of God because it is the will of God is the perfection of moral virtue.

It is a striking fact that whenever the heart of man is pierced by the arrows of the Almighty and his soul is bowed down before the Majesty of heaven, whenever he begins to feel the awful burden of his guilt and his conscience is agitated over his fearful accountabilities and how they are to be met, his inquiry always is "Lord, what wilt Thou have me to do?" Everyone who has been taught of God knows this to be true. There is therefore a revealed testimony in every renewed heart to the righteousness of God's rule and the reality of its obligation. This is the basic principle of Christian fidelity and fortitude. Under its influence the regenerate soul has only one inquiry in reference to any proposed enterprise: Is it the will of God? Satisfied with this, his heart tells him it must be done. Difficulties, hardships, dangers, death present no obstacle; onward he presses in the path marked out for him by the will of his Father. Obedience to that is his only responsibility.

The whole question of man's responsibility is resolved thus: Has God revealed, has God commanded? It must be grounded on the simple authority of the Most High. God neither reveals what is untrue nor commands what is unjust; therefore the first principle of our moral duty is to know, acknowledge and perform the divine will as the ultimate fact in the government of God over us. This question must be resolved altogether irrespective of the state into which the fall has brought man; otherwise God must cease to be God and the creature must sit in judgment on his Creator. But men in the enmity of their carnal mind and the pride of their heart dare to sit in judgment upon the rule God has given them, measuring it by how far they consider it suitable to their condition, how far it complies with their ability, how far it commends itself to their reason— which is the very essence of unbelief and rebellion, the opposite of faith and obedience. Responsibility rests not upon anything in the creature, but on the authority of God who has made known His will to us. Responsibility is our obligation to respond to God's will.

We turn next to consider the moral agency of man. Since God supplied all other creatures with faculties suited to them and abilities to fill their several purposes and to attain their different ends (as fish to swim in water, and birds to fly in the air), so He was no less gracious to man. He who did not deny capacity to His lower creatures did not withhold it from the noblest of His earthly works. How could God have pronounced him "very good" (Gen. 1:31) if he lacked the natural capacity to fulfill the end of his creation? As he was to be subject to moral government, man was endowed with moral agency. Man then has been fitted to serve his Maker, because he has been invested with faculties suited to the substance of the divine commands; therefore it is our certain duty to obey whatever laws God gives us.

In amplifying what has just been said, we must consider the question What is the essence of moral agency? The answer is rational intelligence. If man was incapable of comparing ideas, of marking their agreement or difference to draw conclusions and infer results of conduct, he would not be a moral agent. That is to say, he would not be under a law or revealed will and liable to punishment for its violation or reward for its obedience. We do not treat infants or idiots as subjects of moral government, nor do we regard brute beasts as responsible moral agents. The unhappy maniac is pitied, not blamed. But something more than a capacity to reason is included in the idea of moral agency; there are processes of reason, such as a mathematical demonstration, which contain no moral character.

Man's Power of Choice

To will is an act of the mind directing its thoughts to the production of an action and thereby exerting its power to produce it. The faculty of the will is that power or principle of the mind by which it is capable of choosing. An act of the will is simply a choice. When the herdsmen of Abraham and his nephew quarreled, the patriarch proposed a separation and graciously offered the young man his choice of the whole land. "Then Lot chose him all the plain of Sodom." What does that choice signify? He took a view of the different localities, observed their relative features, balanced in his mind their respective advantages and disadvantages; and that which pleased him best offered the most powerful motive or incentive, and so was his choice. Such power of choice is necessary to constitute moral agency. Anyone who is physically forced to perform an act contrary to his desires, be it good or bad, is not accountable for it.

Conscience is a moral sense which discerns between moral good and evil, perceiving the difference between worthiness and blamableness, reward and punishment. A moral agent is one who has a capacity for being influenced in his actions by moral inducements or motives exhibited to the understanding or reason, so as to engage to a conduct agreeable to the moral faculties. That such a faculty exists within us is witnessed to by the consciousness of men the world over. There is an inward monitor from whose authority there is no escape, ever accusing or excusing. When its authority is defied, sooner or later conscience smites the transgressor with deep remorse and causes him to shrink from the anticipation of a reckoning to come. In a healthy state man recognizes the claims made by his moral faculty to supreme dominion over him. Thus the Creator has placed within our own beings His vice-regent, ever testifying to our responsibility to render obedience to Him.

Man's responsibility does not rest on anything within himself, but is based solely upon God's rights over him—His right to command, His right to be obeyed. The faculties of intelligence, volition and conscience merely qualify man to discharge his responsibility. In addition to these faculties of his soul, man has also been given strength or power to meet the requirements of his Maker. God originally made him "upright" (Eccles. 7:29) and placed within him holy tendencies which perceived the glory of God, a heart which responded to His excellence. Man was made in the image of God, after His likeness (Gen. 1:27); in other words, he was "created in righteousness and true holiness" (Eph. 4:24). Man's understanding was spiritually enlightened, his will rightly inclined; therefore he was capacitated to love the Lord his God with all his faculties and to render Him sinless obedience. Thus was he fitted to discharge his responsibility.

How was it possible for such a creature—so richly endowed by his Creator, so "very good" in his being, so capacitated to love and serve his Maker—to fall? It was possible because he was not constituted immutable, that is, incapable of any change. Creaturehood and mutability (liability to change) are correlated terms. Having been given everything necessary to constitute him a moral agent, everything which fitted him to meet the divine requirements, man was made the subject of moral government. A rule of action was set before him, a rule which was vested with sanctions: reward for obedience, punishment for disobedience. Man then was put on probation under a covenant of works. He was duly tried, his fealty to God being tested by Satan. Man deliberately cast off his allegiance to God, rejected His authority, preferred the creature to his Creator and thereby fell from his original estate.

It needs to be pointed out—for in some circles of professing Christians it is quite unknown—that when God placed Adam under the covenant of works and put him on probation, he acted not simply as a private individual but as a public person, as the federal head, as the legal representative and father of all his posterity. Such was the constitution which it pleased the Lord to appoint to the human race at the beginning of its history; and whether we can or cannot perceive the propriety and righteousness of such an arrangement, no spiritual mind will doubt its wisdom or justice once he is satisfied it is definitely revealed in Holy Writ. Had Adam survived his testing and remained loyal to his Ruler, the whole of his posterity would have shared his reward. Instead, he rebelled and sinned; in consequence, "by the offence of one judgment came upon all men to condemnation; . . . by one man's disobedience many were made sinners" (Rom. 5:18-19); "in Adam all die" (1 Cor. 15:22).

As the result of our federal head's transgression, we are born into this world depraved creatures, unable to render acceptable obedience to the divine law. But the fall has neither changed man's relationship to God nor canceled his responsibility. He is still a subject of the divine government, still a moral agent, still accountable for his actions, still required to love and serve the Lord his God. God has not lost His right to enforce His just demands, though man has lost his power to meet them; depravity does not annul obligation. A human creditor may without the slightest injustice sue a prodigal debtor who has squandered his substance in riotous living. How much more so the divine Creditor! The entrance of sin has neither weakened God's right to demand subjection from His creatures nor invalidated their obligation to discharge their duty.

In seeking to supply solution to the problem of how one who is morally impotent can be justly held to be fully accountable to God, before we endeavor to point out more clearly the exact nature of that impotence (what it does not and what it does consist of), we feel it necessary to further amplify the fact that we must first throw upon this problem the light which is furnished by the relationship which exists between the Creator and the creature, between God and fallen man. Unless we follow this order we are certain to go wrong. It is only in God's light we can ever "see light." God inhabits eternity; man is but a thing of time. Since God is both before and above man, we must start with God in our thoughts and descend to man, and not start with the present condition of fallen man and then seek to think backward to God.

Rights of God over Man

That upon which we must first concentrate is not the rights of man but the rights of God, the rights of God over man. The relation in which the Creator stands to His creatures makes them, in the strictest sense, His property. The Almighty has an absolute right to appropriate and control the products of His own omnipotence and will. Observe how the psalmist ascribes the supremacy of God to the dependence of all things upon Him for their original existence. "For the Lord is a great God, and a great King above all gods. In his hand are the deep places of the earth: the strength of the hills is his also. The sea is his, and he made it: and his hands formed the dry land. O come, let us worship and bow down: let us kneel before the Lord our maker. For he is our God; and we are the people of his pasture, and the sheep of his hand" (Ps. 95:3-7).

Since creation itself gives the Most High an absolute right to the disposal of His creatures, His constant preservation of them continually augments His title. To keep in being calls for the exercise of power no less than to create out of nothing. To God as Creator we owe our original existence; to God as Preserver we are indebted for our continued existence. Upon this sure foundation of creation and preservation God possesses an unquestionable and inalienable propriety in all His creatures, and consequently they are under a corresponding obligation to acknowledge His dominion. Their dependence upon Him for past, present and continued existence makes it a matter of imperative duty to submit to His authority. From the fact that we are His property it follows that His will is our law. "Shall the thing formed say to him that formed it, Why hast thou made me thus?" (Rom. 9:20). God's right to govern us is the necessary consequence of the mutual relations existing between Creator and creatures.

The dominion of God was not adjusted with reference to man, but man was constituted with reference to it. That is to say, it pleased the Lord to appoint and institute a system of moral government, and accordingly He constituted man a moral agent, fitted to His requirements. Man was endowed with understanding, conscience, affections and will, capable of bearing the image of his Maker's holiness, of appreciating the distinctions between right and wrong, of feeling the supremacy of moral law. To such beings God sustains the relation of Ruler, for a moral creature is necessarily the subject of obligation. It must seek the law of its being beyond itself; the ultimate standard of its conduct must be found in a superior will to which it is responsible. To all created intelligences the authority of their Creator is absolute, complete and final. Thus the will of God, now expressed, is to them the sole standard of moral obligation. To deny this would be to make the creature independent.

The essential elements which constitute all true government were present when God placed man in Eden: there was competent authority, a rule of action proclaimed, and a suitable sanction to enforce that rule. As we have pointed out, the relationship obtaining between God and His creatures is such as to invest Him with an absolute right to exact obedience from them. As dependence is the very condition of his being, man possesses no authority to move, to exert a single faculty or to lose a single quality without evoking the divine displeasure. So absolutely is the creature the property of its Maker that it has no right to think its own thoughts or indulge its own inclinations. Moral agents must act, but their actions must be determined and regulated by the will of their Maker. "And the Lord God commanded the man, saying, Of every tree of the garden thou mayest freely eat" (Gen. 2:16); without the grant, it would have been an act of theft for Adam to partake of any of them!

J. H. Thornwell stated:

A creature has no more right to act than it has power to be, without the consent of the Almighty. Dependence, absolute, complete, inalienable is the law of its existence. Whatever it performs must be in the way of obedience; there can be no obedience without an indication of the will of a ruler, and no such indication without a government. It is, therefore, undeniably necessary that to justify a creature in acting at all there must be some expression, more or less distinct, direct or indirect of the will of its Creator. As, then, the Almighty, from the very necessity of the case, must will to establish some rule, we are prepared to inquire what kind of government He was pleased to institute.

As we mentioned previously, it was a moral government, of moral creatures, who were placed under revealed law. It was law to which was attached penal sanction, and this in the very nature of the case. In order to enforce His authority as Ruler, in order to make manifest the estimate He places upon His law, God determined that disobedience to that law must be visited with summary punishment. How else could God's hatred of sin be known? Since the moral conduct of a creature is to be regulated with a specific reference to God's authority, unless He allowed it to be a god—uncontrolled, independent—there must be a recognition of His right to command. The actions of a moral creature must proceed from a sense of obligation corresponding to the rights of the Ruler. But there could be no such sense of obligation unless the law was enforced by a penal sanction; for without such, the obedience of the creature would be merely the result of persuasion rather than authority.

Precept without penalty is simply advice, or at most a request; and rewards without punishment are nothing but inducements. Had Adam and Eve been placed under such principles, the result would evidently have been but a system of persuasion and not of authoritative rule (which is precisely what most human government, in the home, the church and the state, has now degenerated into). In such a case their obedience would have been nothing more than pleasing themselves, following the impulse of their own desires, and not submitting to the rightful demands of their Creator; they would have been acting out their own wills and not the will of the Most High. It should be quite plain to the reader that such an (inconceivable) arrangement would have vested the creature with absolute sovereignty, making it a law unto itself, entirely independent of its Maker. The essence of all morality is compliance with the will of God, not because it commends itself to our reason or is agreeable to our disposition, but simply because it is His will.

In order that the will of God may be felt as law and may produce in the creature a corresponding sense of obligation, it must be enforced by a penal sanction. Declared penalty for disobedience upholds the authority of the Creator and keeps prominently in view the responsibility of the creature. It makes clear the just supremacy of the One and the due subordination of the other. The moral sense in man, even in fallen man, bears witness to the rightness of this basic fact. Conscience is a prospective principle; its decisions are by no means final, but are only the prelude of a higher sentence to be pronounced in a higher court. Conscience derives its power from anticipations of the future. It brings before its possessor the dread tribunal of eternal justice and almighty power; it summons us into the awful presence of a right-loving and sin-hating God. It testifies to an ultimate reward for right doing and an ultimate punishment for wrongdoing.

We again quote Thornwell:

When a man of principle braves calumny, reproach and persecution, when he stands unshaken in the discharge of duty and public opposition and private treachery, when no machinations of malice or seductions of flattery can cause him to bend from the path of integrity,—that must be a powerful support through which he can bid defiance to the "storms of fate." He must feel that a strong arm is underneath him; and though the eye of sense can perceive nothing in his circumstances but terror, confusion, and dismay, he sees his mountain surrounded by "chariots of fire and horses of fire," which sustain his soul in unbroken tranquility. In the approbation of his conscience there is lifted up the light of the Divine countenance upon him, and he feels the strongest assurance that all things shall work together for his ultimate good. Conscience anticipates the rewards of the just, and in the conviction which it inspires of Divine protection lays the foundation of heroic fortitude.

When, on the contrary, the remembrance of some fatal crime rankles in the breast, the sinner's dreams are disturbed by invisible ministers of vengeance and the fall of a leaf can strike him with horror; in every shadow he sees a ghost: in every tread he hears an avenger of blood; and in every sound the trump of doom. What is it that invests his conscience with such terrible power to torment? Is there nothing here but the natural operation of a simple and original instinct? Who does not see that the alarm and agitation and fearful forebodings of the sinner arise from the terrors of an offended Judge and insulted Lawgiver. An approving conscience is the consciousness of right, of having done what has been commanded, and of being now entitled to the favor of the Judge. Remorse is the sense of ill-desert. The criminal does not feel that his present pangs are his punishment; it is the future, the unknown and portentous future, that fills him with consternation. He deserves ill, and the dread of receiving it makes him tremble.

Let there be no uncertainty on this point. Were it possible to remove the penalty from the divine law, we should be wresting the scepter from the hands of Deity, divesting Him of power to enforce His just demands, denuding Him of the essential dignity of His character, reducing Him to a mere suppliant at the feet of His creatures. Modern theology (if it deserves to be called theology) presents to men a parody of God, who commands the respect of none, who is disrobed of His august and glorious majesty, who, far from doing His will in the army of heaven and among the inhabitants of the earth, is pictured as a kindly petitioner seeking favors at the hands of worms of the dust. Such a "god" has no powerful voice which shakes the earth and makes guilty rebels quail, but only offers entreaties which may be despised with impunity. Unless God is able to enforce His will He ceases to be God. If He speaks with authority, resistless power stands ready to support His command.

"And the Lord God commanded the man, saying, Of every tree of the garden thou mayest freely eat: but of the tree of the knowledge of good and evil thou shalt not eat of it" (Gen. 2:16-17). There was the original command given to man at the dawn of human history. It surely was uttered in a tone which carried the conviction that it must be obeyed. "For in the day that thou eatest thereof thou shalt surely die." There was the penal sanction enforcing the authority of the Lawgiver, the plainly announced penalty for transgression. Man was not left in ignorance or uncertainty of what would follow the forbidden act. The loss of God's favor, the incurring of His sore displeasure, certain and inescapable destruction would be the portion of the disobedient. And that awful threat was no isolated and exceptional one, but the enunciation of an abiding principle which God has constantly pressed upon men all through His Word: "The soul that sinneth, it shall die"; "The wages of sin is death." Even when the Savior commissioned His servants to go forth and preach the gospel to every creature, He expressly told them to make known that "he that believeth not shall be damned." Such a God is not to be trifled with!

Let us digress for a moment. In view of what has been said above, the discerning reader will hardly need for us to point out to him the unspeakable solemnity, the immeasurable awfulness, the consummate folly of the course followed in the vast majority of the pulpits for many years. Even where the requirements of the moral law have been insisted on, its fearful penal sanction scarcely ever has been pressed. It has either been flatly denied that God will consign to everlasting woe all who have trampled on His commandments and died impenitent of their rebellion, or else a guilty silence has been maintained and in its stead a one-sided portrayal of the divine character presented, all the emphasis being placed on His love and mercy. Disastrous indeed must be the consequence of such a course, and disastrous indeed has it proved. An insulted Deity is now allowing us to reap what we have sown.

Problem of Lawlessness

A law which is not enforced by penalties will not be obeyed. True alike of God's law or man's, God's law will exert very little restraining influence upon the unregenerate if fear of the wrath to come is not definitely before their minds; and the multitude will have little respect for the statutes of the realm once they cease to regard the magistrate with "terror" (Rom. 13:2-4). For generations past there has been scarcely anything from the pulpit to inspire fear of God, and now there is practically no fear of magistracy left. Respect for the divine authority has not been faithfully proclaimed and enforced, and now there is only a mere pretense of respect for human authority. The terrible penalty for disobeying God's law—endless suffering in the lake of fire—has not been plainly and frequently held before those in the pew, and now we are witnessing a miserable parody, a mere formal pretense of enforcing the prescribed penalties for violations of human laws.

During the course of the last century, churchgoers grew less and less afraid of the consequences of breaking God's precepts; now the masses, even children, are less and less afraid of transgressing the laws of our country. Witness not merely the leniency but the utter laxity of most of our magistrates in dismissing offenders either with a warning or a trifling fine; witness the many murderers sentenced to death "with strong recommendation for mercy" and the increasing number of those whose capital punishment is remitted; witness the pathetic spectacle of governments afraid to act firmly, making "appeals" and "requests," instead of using their authority. And what we are now seeing in the civil realm is the inevitable repercussion of what took place in the religious. We sowed the wind; a righteous God is now allowing us to reap the whirlwind. Nor can there be any hope of a return to law and order, either between the nations or in our civil life, until the law of God is again given its proper place in our homes and churches, until the authority of the Lawgiver is respected, until the penalty for breaking His law is proclaimed.

Returning to our more immediate discussion, it should be pointed out that the fall did not to the slightest degree cancel man's responsibility. How could it? Man is just as much under the authority of God now as he was in Eden. He is still as truly the subject of divine command as he ever was, and therefore as much responsible to render perfect and ceaseless obedience to the divine law. The responsibility of man, be he unfallen or fallen, is that of a subject to his sovereign. They who imagine that man's own willful sin has canceled his obligation show how completely darkened is their judgment. Since God continues to be man's rightful Lord and man is His lawful subject, since He still possesses the right to command and we are still under obligation to obey, it should not be thought strange that God deals with man according to this relationship, and actually requires obedience to His law though man is no longer able to give it.

No, the fall of man most certainly has neither annulled nor impaired man's responsibility. Why should it? It was not God who took from man his spiritual strength and deprived him of his ability. Man was originally endowed with power to meet the righteous requirements of his Maker; it was by his own madness and wickedness that he threw away that power. Does a human monarch forfeit his right to demand allegiance from his subjects as soon as they turn rebels? Certainly not. It is his prerogative to demand that they throw down the weapons of their warfare and return to their original loyalty. Has then the King of kings no such right to require that lawless rebels become loyal subjects? We repeat, it was not God who stripped man of original righteousness, for he had lost it before God passed sentence upon him, as his "I was naked" (Gen. 3:10) acknowledged. If inability canceled man's obligation, there would be no sin in the world, and consequently no judgment here or hereafter. For God to allow that fallen creatures be absolved from loving Him with all their hearts would be to abrogate His government.

God's sovereignty and man's responsibility are never confounded in the Scriptures but, from the two trees in the midst of Eden's garden (the "tree of life" and "the tree of knowledge of good and evil" [Gen. 2:9]) onward, are placed in juxtaposition. Human responsibility is the necessary corollary of divine sovereignty. Since God is the Creator, since He is sovereign Ruler over all, and since man is simply a creature and a subject, there is no escape from his accountability to his Maker. For what is man responsible? Man is obligated to answer to the relationship which exists between him and his Creator. He occupies the place of creaturehood, subordination, complete dependence; therefore he must acknowledge God's dominion, submit to His authority, and love Him with all his heart and strength. The discharge of human responsibility is simply to recognize God's rights and act accordingly, rendering His unquestionable due.

Man's Accountability to God

Responsibility is entirely a matter of relationship and the discharge of those obligations which that relationship entails. When a man takes a wife he enters into a new relationship and incurs new obligations, and his marital responsibility lies in the fulfillment of those obligations. If a child is given to him a further relationship is involved with added obligations (to both his wife and child), and his parental responsibility consists of the faithful meeting of those obligations. Once it is known who God is and what is man's relationship to Him, the question of his responsibility is settled once for all. God is our Owner and Governor, possessed of absolute authority over us, and this must be acknowledged by us in deed as well as word. Thus we are responsible to be in complete subjection to the will of our Maker and Lord, to employ in His service the faculties He has given us, to use the means He has appointed, and to improve the opportunities and advantages He had provided us. Our whole duty is to glorify God.

From the above definition it should be crystal clear that the fall did not and could not to the slightest degree cancel or impair human responsibility. The fall has not altered the fundamental relationship subsisting between Creator and creature. God is the Owner of sinful man as truly and as fully as He was of sinless man. God is still our Sovereign and we are still His subjects. God's absolute dominion over us pertains as strictly now as it did in Eden. Though man has lost his power to obey, God has not lost His right to demand. To argue that inability cancels responsibility is the height of absurdity. Because an intoxicated employee is incapable of performing his duties, is his master deprived of the right to demand their accomplishment? Man cannot blame God for the wretched condition in which he now finds himself. The entire onus rests on the creature, for his moral impotence is the immediate effect of his own wrongdoing.

God's right to command and man's obligation to give perfect and perpetual obedience remain unshaken. God gave man his "substance" (Luke 15), but he spent it in riotous living; nevertheless God may justly challenge His own. If an earthly master gives a servant money and sends him to purchase supplies, may he not lawfully demand those supplies even if that servant spends the money in debauchery and gambling? God supplied Adam with a suitable stock, but he trifled it away. Surely then God is not to suffer because of the creature's folly; He should not be deprived of His right because of man's crime. The fact that man is a spiritual embezzler cannot destroy God's authority to require what the creature cannot be excused from. A debtor who cannot pay the debts which he has incurred remains under the obligation of paying. God not only possesses the right to demand from man the debt of obedience; from Genesis 3 to the last chapter of the New Testament He exercises and enforces that right and will yet make it publicly manifest before the assembled universe.

Though it be true that man himself is entirely to blame for the wretched spiritual condition in which he now finds himself, that the guilt of his depravity and powerlessness lies at his own door, yet we must not lose sight of the fact that his very impotence is a penal infliction, a divine judgment upon his original rebellion. Moral inability is the necessary effect of disobedience, for sin is essentially destructive, being opposed to all that is holy. God has so ordered it that the effects which sin has produced in man furnish a powerful witness to and an unmistakable demonstration of the exceeding sinfulness of sin and the dreadfulness of the malady which it produces. Sin not only defiles but enervates. It not only makes man obnoxious in the pure eyes of his Maker, but it saps man of his original strength to use his faculties right; and the more he now indulges in sin the more he increases his inability to walk uprightly.

Further light is cast on the problem of fallen man's responsibility by obtaining a right view of the precise nature of his inability. Let us begin by pointing out what it does not consist of. First, the moral inability of fallen man does not lie in the absence of any of those faculties which are necessary to constitute him a moral agent. By his transgression man lost both his spiritual purity and power, but he lost none of his original faculties. Fallen man possesses every faculty with which unfallen man was endowed. He is still a rational creature. He has an understanding to think with, affections capable of being exercised, a conscience to discern between right and wrong, a will to make choice with. Because man is in possession of such capacities he has faculties suited to the substance of the divine commands. Because he is a moral agent he is under moral government, and must yet render an account to the supreme Governor.

At this point notice must be taken of an error which obtains in the minds of some, tending to obscure and undermine the truth of fallen man s unimpaired responsibility. God declared that in the day Adam ate of the forbidden fruit he should "surely die," which has been wrongly understood to mean that his spirit would be extinguished and that, consequently, while the natural man possesses a soul he has no spirit, and cannot have one until he is born again. This is quite wrong. In Scripture "death" signifies separation and never annihilation. At physical death the soul is not exterminated but separated from the body. The spiritual death of Adam was not the extinction of any part of his being, but the severance of his fellowship with a holy God. In consequence Adam's descendants are born into this world "dead in trespasses and sins," which is defined as "being alienated from the life of God through the ignorance that is in them, because of the blindness of their heart" (Eph. 4:18).

When the prodigal's father said, "This my son was dead, and is alive again" (Luke 15:24), he most certainly did not mean that the son had ceased to exist, but simply that the prodigal had been "in the far country" and had now returned. The lake of fire into which the wicked are cast is termed the second death (Rev. 20:14) because they are "punished with everlasting destruction from the presence of the Lord, and from the glory of his power" (2 Thess. 1:9). That the natural man is possessed of a spirit is clear from "the Lord which . . . formeth the spirit of man within him" (Zech. 12:1); "What man knoweth the things of a man, save the spirit of man which is in him?" (1 Cor. 2:11); "The spirit shall return unto God who gave it" (Eccles. 12:7). It is a serious mistake to say that when Adam died in Eden any portion of his tripartite nature ceased to exist. Fallen man, we repeat, possesses all the faculties which unfallen man had.

When the Scriptures affirm "They that are in the flesh cannot please God" (Rom. 8:8) it is not because these lack the necessary faculties. That "cannot" must be understood in a way which comports fully with fallen man's responsibility, otherwise we should be guilty of making one verse contradict another. The "cannot" of Romans 8:8 (and similar passages) is in no way analogous to the "cannot walk" of a man who has lost his legs, or the "cannot see" of one who is deprived of his eyes. In such cases the individuals "cannot" because they do not have the requisite faculties or organs. A person who was devoid of such members at his birth could not possibly be held accountable for the non-exercise of them. But the moral impotence of the sinner is far otherwise. He does possess moral faculties, and the reason he fails to use them for the glory of God is solely because of his hatred of Him, because of the corruption of his nature, the enmity of his mind, the perversity of his will; and for these he is responsible.

For a man to be so enslaved by strong drink that he cannot help getting inebriated, far from excusing him, adds to his condemnation. For a man to give way to speaking what is untrue, forming the habit of telling falsehoods until he becomes such a confirmed liar that he is incapable of uttering the truth, only evidences the awful depths of his depravity. But ponder carefully the nature of his incapability. It is not because he has lost any faculty, for he still possesses the organs of speech, but because he has sunk so low that he can no longer use those organs to good purpose. Thus it is with the natural man and his incapability of pleasing his Maker. Man is endowed with moral faculties but he perverts them, puts them to wrong use. He has the same heart for loving God as for hating Him, the same members for serving Him as for disobeying Him.

Stephen Charnock said:

It is strange if God should invite the trees or beasts to repent, because they have no foundation in their nature to entertain commandments and invitations to obedience and repentance; for trees have no sense and beasts have no reason to discern the difference between good and evil. But God addresseth Himself to men that have senses open to objects, understanding to know, wills to move, affections to embrace objects. These understandings are open to anything but that which God doth command, their wills can will anything but that which God doth propose. The commandment is proportioned to their rational faculty and the faculty is proportioned to the excellency of the command.

We have affections, as love and desire. In the commands of loving God and loving our neighbor there is only a change of the object of our affections required; the faculties are not weakly but by viciousness of nature, which is of our own introduction. It is strange, therefore, that we should excuse ourselves and pretend we are not to be blamed because God's command is impossible to be observed, when the defect lies not in the want of a rational foundation, but in our own giving up ourselves to the flesh and the love of it, and in willful refusal of applying our faculties to their proper objects, when we can employ those faculties with all vehemence about those things which have no commerce with the Gospel.

This is a suitable place for us to mention and correct a mistake which occurs in some of our earlier writings. Lacking the light which God has now vouchsafed us, we then taught (1) that fallen man still possessed a natural ability to render to God the obedience which He requires, though he lacks the necessary moral ability; and (2) that because man is possessed of such natural ability he is a responsible creature. The first mistake was really more a matter of terms than anything else, for all that we meant to signify by "natural ability" was the possession of faculties which capacitated man to act as a moral agent; nevertheless, as wrong terms conduce to wrong ideas we must correct them. The second was an error in doctrine, due to our ignorance. In this present work we have shown that the basis of human responsibility consists not in anything in man, but rather in his relationship to God, and that the faculties which make him a moral agent merely equip him to discharge his responsibility.

Chapter 9
Affirmation

Many able writers, in their efforts to solve the problem presented by the moral impotence and yet the moral responsibility of fallen man, have stressed the distinction between natural and moral ability and inability. They have not seen how a man could be held accountable for his actions unless he was, in some sense, capable of performing his duty. That capability they have ascribed to his being in possession of all the faculties requisite for the performance of obedience to the divine law. But it is now clear to us that these men employed the wrong term when they designated this possession of faculties a "natural ability," for the simple but sufficient reason that fallen man has lost the power or strength to use those faculties right; it is surely a misuse of terms to predicate "ability" in one who is without strength. To affirm that the natural man possesses ability of any sort is really a denial of his total depravity.

In the second place, it should be pointed out that the moral inability of the natural man is not brought about by any external compulsion. It is an utterly erroneous idea to suppose that the natural man possesses or may possess a genuine desire and determination to do that which is pleasing to God and to abstain from what is displeasing to Him, but that a power outside himself thwarts him and obliges him to act contrary to his inclinations. Were such the case, man would be neither a moral agent nor a responsible creature. If some physical law operated upon man (like, that which regulates the planets), if some external violence (like the wind) carried men forward where they did not desire to go, they would be exempted from guilt. Those who are compelled to do what they are decidedly averse to cannot be justly held accountable for such actions.

Influence of Motives on the Will

One of the essential elements of moral agency is that the agent acts without external compulsion, in accord with his own desires. The mind must be capable of considering the motives to action which are placed before it and of choosing its own course—by "motives" we mean those reasons or inducements which influence to choice and action. Thus that which would be a powerful motive in the view of one mind would be no motive at all in the view of another. The offer of a bribe would be sufficient inducement to move one judge to decide a case contrary to evidence and law; to another such an offer, far from being a motive for wrongdoing, would be highly repellent. The temptation presented by Potiphar's wife, which was firmly resisted by Joseph, would have been an inducement sufficiently powerful to ruin many a youth of less purity of heart.

It should be quite evident that no external motive (inducement or consideration) can have any influence over our choices and actions except so far as they make an appeal to inclinations already existing within us. The affections of the heart act freely and spontaneously: in the very nature of the case we cannot be compelled either to love or to hate any object. Neither an infant nor an idiot is capable of weighing motives or of discerning moral values; therefore they are not accountable creatures, amenable to law. But because man, though fallen and under the dominion of sin, is still a rational being, possessed of the power to ponder the motives set before his mind and to decide good and evil, he is fully accountable, for he freely chooses that which, on the whole, he most prefers. Moral agency can only be destroyed by a force from without obliging man to act contrary to his nature and inclinations.

There is nothing outside of man which imposes on him any necessity of sinning or which prevents his turning from sin to holiness. There is no force brought to bear immediately on man's power of volition, or even on the connection between his volitions and his actions, which obliges him to follow the course he does. No, what man does ordinarily he does voluntarily or spontaneously in the uncontrolled exercise of his own faculties. No compulsion whatever is imposed on him. He does evil, nothing but evil, simply because he chooses to do so; the only immediate and direct cause of his doing evil is that he so wills it. Therefore since man is a responsible creature who, without any external power forcing him to act contrary to his desires, freely rejects the good and chooses the evil, he must be held accountable for his criminal conduct.

What has been pointed out considerably relieves the difficulty presented by the impotence of fallen man to meet the just requirements of God. If the reader will carefully ponder the case it should be apparent to him that the problem of human inability and accountability is by no means so formidable as it appears at first sight. The case of the fallen creature is vastly altered once it is clear what his impotence does not consist of. It makes a tremendous difference that his inability to obey his Maker does not lie in the absence of those faculties by which obedience is performed. So too the complexion of the case is radically changed when we perceive that man is not the victim of a hostile power outside himself which forces him to act contrary to his own desires and inclinations.

Grounds for Man's Blame

It will thus be evident that far from fallen man being an object of pity because of his moral impotence, he is justly to be blamed for the course which he pursues. We do not condemn a legless man because he is unable to walk, but rightly commiserate with him. We do not censure a sightless man for not admiring the beauties of nature; rather our compassion goes out to him. But how different is the case of the natural man in connection with his firm obligations to serve and glorify his rightful Lord! He is in possession of all the requisite faculties, but he voluntarily misuses them, deliberately following a course of madness and wickedness; for that he is most certainly culpable. His guiltiness will appear yet more plainly in what follows, when we understand what his moral impotence does consist of, when we consider the several elements which comprise it.

A further word needs to be added on the error of affirming that fallen man possesses a natural "ability" to obey God. Most of the writers who affirm this (Calvinists) take the ground that all the natural man lacks in order to perform that which is pleasing to God is a willingness to do so; that since his mental and moral endowments are admirably suited to the substance of the divine commandments, and since he is still possessed of every faculty which is required for the discharge of his duty, he could obey God if he would. But this is far from being the case. The condition of fallen man is much worse than that. He not only will not, but he cannot please God. Such is the emphatic and unequivocal teaching of Holy Writ, and it must be held fast by us at all costs, no matter what difficulties it may seem to involve. Yet we are fully convinced that this cannot, does not in the least, annul man's responsibility or make him any less blameworthy than was sinless Adam in committing his first offense.

"Unto them that are defiled and unbelieving is nothing pure; but even their mind and conscience is defiled" (Titus 1:15). In the unregenerate the mind and conscience are under an inherent and universal incapacity to form a right judgment or come to a right decision in regard to things pertaining to God, and as pertaining to Him. It is not merely that they are in the condition of one with a thick veil before his eyes, while the eyes themselves are sound and whole; rather they are like one whose eyes are diseased—weakened, decayed in their very internal organism. A diseased physical eye may be incapable of giving safe direction. But the eyes of fallen man's heart and understanding are so seriously affected that they cannot receive or even tolerate any spiritual light at all, until the great Physician heals them.

The solemn and terrible fact is that the brighter and more glorious is the divine light shed on the unregenerate, the more offensive and unbearable it is to them. The eyes of our understanding are radically diseased, and it is the understanding—under false views and erroneous estimates of things— which misleads the affections and the will. How, then, can we with the slightest propriety affirm that man still possesses a "natural ability" to receive God's truth to the saving of his soul? In man as created there was a perfect adaptation of faculties and a capability of receiving the divine testimony. But in fallen man, though there is a suitableness in the essential nature of his faculties to receive the testimony of God—so that his case is far superior to that of the brute beast—yet his ability to use those faculties and actually to receive God's testimony for suitable ends is completely deranged and destroyed.

Disorganization of Man's Being

The entrance of sin into man has done far more than upset his poise and disorder his affections. It has corrupted and disorganized his whole being. His intellectual faculties are so impaired and debased that his understanding is quite incapable of discerning spiritual things in a spiritual manner. His heart (including the will), which is the practical principle of operation, is "desperately wicked" and in a state of "blindness" (Eph. 4:18). The mind of fallen man is not only negatively ignorant, but positively opposed to light and convictions. To say that the natural man could please God if he would is false. His impotence is insurmountable, for he lacks the nature or disposition to will good. Therefore many men have greatly erred in supposing that the faculties of man are as capable now of receiving the testimony of God as they were before the fall.

Unwillingness is not all that the Scriptures predicate of fallen man. They declare sin has so corrupted his being that he is completely incapable of holy perceptions; it has utterly disabled him to perform spiritual acts. Moses told the people of Israel, "Ye have seen all that the Lord did before your eyes in the land of Egypt unto Pharaoh, and unto all his servants, and unto all his land; the great temptations which thine eyes have seen, the signs, and those great miracles: yet the Lord hath not given you a heart to perceive, and eyes to see, and ears to hear, unto this day" (Deut. 29:2-4). The faculties were there, but the people had not obtained power from God to perceive. Earlier Moses had said, "And the Lord heard the voice of your words, when ye spoke unto me; and the Lord said unto me, I have heard the voice of the words of this people, which they have spoken unto thee: they have well said all that they have spoken. O that there were such an heart in them, that they would fear me, and keep all my commandments always, that it might be well with them, and with their children forever" (Deut. 5:28-29). The faculties were there, but they lacked the spiritual power to use them. The unregenerate man is utterly disabled by indwelling sin in all the faculties of his spirit and soul and body from thinking, feeling or doing any spiritual good toward God.

Yet these facts do not to the slightest degree destroy or even lessen man s responsibility to glorify his Maker. This will more fully appear as we now consider what man's inability actually consists of. First, it is a voluntary inability. It was so originally. Adam acted freely when he ate of the forbidden fruit, and in consequence he lost his native holiness and became in bondage to evil. Nor can his descendants justly murmur at their inheriting the depravity of their first parents and being made answerable for their inability to will or to do good, as part of the forfeiture penalty due the first transgression; their moral impotence consists of their own voluntary continuation of Adam's offense. The entire history of sin lies in inclination and self-determination. It must not be supposed for a moment that after the first sin of Adam all self-determination ceased.

W. G. Shedd stated:

Original sin, as corruption of nature in each individual, is only the continuation of the first inclining away from God. The self-determination of the human will from God the creature, as an ultimate end, did not stop short with the act in Eden, but goes right onward to every individual of Adam's posterity, until regeneration reverses it. As progressive sanctification is the continuation of that holy self-determination of the human will which begins in its regeneration by the Holy Spirit, so the progressive depravation of the natural man is the continuation of that sinful self-determination of the human will which began in Adam's transgression.

The very origin and nature of man's inability for good demonstrates that it cannot annul his responsibility; it was self-induced and is now self -perpetuated. Far from human depravity being a calamity for which we are to be pitied, it is a crime for which we are rightly to be blamed. Far from sin being a weakness or innocent infirmity rising from some defect of creation, it is a hostile power, a vicious enmity against God. The endowments of the creature placed him under lasting obligation to his Creator, and that obligation cannot be canceled by any subsequent action of the creature. If man has deliberately destroyed his power, he has not destroyed his obligation. God does no man wrong in requiring from him what he cannot now perform, for by his own deliberate act of disobedience man deprived himself and his posterity of that power; and his posterity consent to Adam's act of disobedience by deliberately choosing and following a similar course of wickedness.

But how can man be said to act voluntarily when he is impelled to do evil by his own lusts? Because he freely chooses the evil. This calls for a closer definition of freedom or voluntariness of action. A free agent is one who is at liberty to act according to his own choice, without compulsion or restraint. Has not fallen man this liberty? Does he, in any instance, break God's law by compulsion, against his inclinations? If it were true that the effect of human depravity is to destroy free agency and accountability, it would necessarily follow that the more depraved or vicious a man becomes the less capable he is of sinning, and that the most depraved of all commit the least sin of any. This is too absurd to need refutation.

Though on the one hand it is a fact that fallen man is the slave of sin and the captive of the devil, yet on the other it is equally true that he is still a voluntary and accountable agent. Man has not lost the essential power of choice, or he would cease to be man. Though in one sense he is impelled hellward by the downward trend of his depravity, yet he elects to sin, consenting to it. Though the rectitude of our will is lost, nevertheless we still act spontaneously. "The soul of the wicked desireth evil" (Prov. 21:10), and for that he is to be blamed. If a man picked your pocket and, when arrested, said, "I could not help myself; I have a thieving disposition, and I am obliged to act according to my nature," his judge would reply, "All the more reason why you should be in prison."

Because fallen man possesses the power of choice and is a rational creature, he is obligated to make a wise and good choice. The fault lies

entirely at his own door that he does not do so, for he deliberately chooses the evil. "They have chosen their own ways, and their soul delighteth
in their abominations. I also will choose their delusions, and will bring
their fears upon them; because when I called, none did answer; when I
spoke, they did not hear: but they did evil before mine eyes, and chose
that in which I delighted not" (Isa. 66:3-4). The bondage of the will to
sinful inclinations neither destroys voluntariness nor responsibility, for
the enslaved will is still a self-determining faculty and, therefore, under
inescapable obligations to choose what man knows to be right. That very
bondage is culpable, for it proceeds from self and not from God. Though
man is the slave of sin it is a voluntary servitude, and therefore it is inexcusable.

The will is biased by the disposition of the heart: as the heart is, so
the will acts. A holy will has a holy bias and therefore is under a moral
necessity of exerting holy volitions: "A good tree cannot bring forth evil
fruit." But a sinful will has a sinful bias because it has an evil disposition
and therefore is under a moral necessity of exerting sinful volitions. But
let it be pointed out once more that the evil disposition of man's will is
not the effect of some original defect in the creature, for God made man
"upright." No, his sinful disposition is the abiding self-determination of
the human will. Its origin is due to the misuse Adam made of his freedom, and its continuation results from the unceasing self-determination
of every one of his posterity. Each man perpetuates and prolongs the evil
started by his first parents.

Because man must act according to the state of his heart, does this destroy his freedom? Certainly not, for acting according to his heart simply
means doing as he pleases. And doing as we please is the very thing in
which all free agency consists. The pulse can beat and the limbs can act
in bodily disorders, whether we will or no. We would, with good reason,
consider ourselves unfairly dealt with if we were blamed for such actions;
nor does God hold us accountable for them. A good man's pulse may beat
as irregularly in sickness as the worst villain's in the world; his hands
may strike convulsively those who seek to hold him still. For such actions as these we are not accountable because they have no moral value.
No evil inclination of ours nor the lack of a good one is necessary in order
to do them; they are independent of us.

If all our actions were involuntary and out of our power, in no way necessarily connected with our disposition, our temper of mind, our choice,
then we should not be accountable creatures or the subjects of moral
government. If a good tree could bring forth evil fruit and a corrupt tree
good fruit, if a good man out of the good treasure of his heart could bring
forth evil things, and an evil man out of his evil treasure good things, the
tree could never be known by its fruit. In such a case, all moral distinctions would be at an end and moral government would cease to be, for
men could no longer be dealt with according to their works—rewarded
for the good and punished for the evil. The only man who is justly held

accountable, rewardable or punishable is one whose actions are properly his own, dictated by himself and impossible without his consent.

Here, then, is the answer to the objection that if fallen man is obliged to act according to the evil bias of his heart, he cannot rightly be termed a free agent. Necessity and choice are incompatible. Any inability to act otherwise than agreeably to our own minds would be an inability to act other than as free agents. But that necessity which arises from, or rather consists in, the temper and choice of the agent himself is the very opposite of acting against his nature and freedom. The sinner acts freely because he consents, even when irresistibly influenced by his evil lusts. Of Christ we read, "The spirit driveth him into the wilderness" (Mark 1:12), which indicates a forcible motion and powerful influence; yet of this same action we are also told, "Then was Jesus led up of the spirit into the wilderness" (Matt. 4:1), which plainly signifies His freedom of action. So too the Christian is both drawn and taught of God (John 6:44-45). Liberty of will and the victorious efficacy of divine grace are united together.

Second, fallen man's inability is moral, not physical or constitutional. Unless this is clearly perceived we shall be inclined to turn our impotence into an excuse or ground of self-extenuation. Man will be ready to say, "Even though I possess the requisite faculties for the discharge of my duty, if I am powerless I cannot be blamed for not doing it." A person who is paralyzed possesses all the members of his body, but he lacks the physical power to use them; and no one condemns him for his helplessness. It needs to be made plain that when the sinner is said to be morally and spiritually "without strength," his case is entirely different from that of one who is paralyzed physically. The normal or ordinary natural man is not without either mental or physical strength to use his talents. What he lacks is a good heart, a disposition to love and serve God, a desire to please Him; and for that lack he is justly blamable.

The mental and moral faculties with which man is endowed, despite their impaired condition, place him under moral obligation to love and serve his Creator. The illustrious character and perfections of God make it unmistakably clear that He is infinitely worthy of being loved and served; therefore we are bound to love Him, which is what a good heart essentially does. There is no way of evading the plain teaching of Christ on this subject in the parable of the talents: "Thou oughtest therefore to have put my money to the exchangers, and then at my coming I should have received mine own with usury" (Matt. 25:27). In the light of the immediate context, this clearly means that man ought to have had a heart to invest to the best advantage (use right) the talents which were committed to him.

The inability of the natural man to meet the holy and just requirements of God consists in the opposition of his heart to Him because of the presence and prevalence of a vicious and corrupt disposition. Men know that God does not desire from them a selfish and wicked heart, and they also know that He has the right to require from them a good and obedient heart. To deny that God has the right to require a holy and good heart from fallen man would be tantamount to saying He had no right to require anything from them; then it would follow that they were incapable of sinning against Him. For if God had no right to require anything from man, he would not be guilty of disobedience against Him. If God has no right to require a good heart from man, then He has no right to require him to do anything which he is unwilling to do, which would render him completely innocent.

A child has no right to complain against a parent for requiring him to do that which he has faculties to perform, but for which he has no heart. A servant has no right to murmur against a master for reasonably requiring him to do that which his endowments fit him to perform, but for which he is unwilling. A subject has no right to find fault with a ruler for requiring him to perform that which the good of his country demands, and which he is capacitated to render, merely because he lacks the disposition to do it. All human authority presupposes a right to require that of men which they are qualified to perform, even though they may have no heart for it. How much less reason, then, have those who are the subjects of divine authority to complain of being required to do that which their faculties fit them for but which their hearts hate. God has the same supreme right to command cordial and universal obedience from Adam's posterity as He has from the holy angels in heaven.

For the sake of those who desire additional insight on the relation of man's inability to his responsibility, we feel we must further consider this difficult but important (perhaps to some, abstruse and dry) aspect of our subject. Light on it has come to us "here a little, there a little"; but it is our duty to share with others the measure of understanding vouchsafed us. We have sought to show that the problem we are wrestling with appears much less formidable when once the precise nature of man's impotence is properly defined. It is due neither to the absence of requisite faculties for the performance of duty nor to any force from without which compels him to act contrary to his nature and inclinations. Instead, his bondage to sin is voluntary; he freely chooses the evil. Second, it is a moral inability, and not physical or constitutional.

In saying that the spiritual impotence of fallen man is a moral one, we mean that it consists of an evil heart, of enmity against God. The man has no affection for his Maker, no will to please Him, but instead an inveterate desire and determination to please himself and have his own way, at all costs. It is therefore a complete misrepresentation of the facts to picture fallen man as a being who wishes to serve God but who is prevented from doing so by his depraved nature; to infer that he genuinely endeavors to keep His law but is hindered by indwelling sin. The fact is that he always acts from his evil heart and not against it. Man is not well disposed toward his Creator, but ill disposed. No matter what change occurs in his circumstances, be it from poverty to wealth, sickness to health, or vice versa, man remains a rebel—perverse, stubborn, wicked—with no desire to be any better, hating the light and loving the darkness.

It therefore follows that man's voluntary and moral inability to serve and glorify God is, third, a criminal one. As we have pointed out, a wicked heart is a thing of an entirely different order from weak eyesight, a bad memory or paralyzed limbs. No man is to blame for physical infirmities, providing they have not been self-induced by sinful conduct. But a wicked heart is a moral evil, indeed the sum of all evil, for it hates God and is opposed to our neighbors, instead of loving them as we are required. To say that a sinner cannot change or improve his heart is only to say he cannot help being a most vile and inexcusable wretch. To be unalterably in love with sin, far from rendering it less sinful, makes it more so. Surely it is self-evident that the more wicked a man's heart is, the more evil and blameworthy he is. The only other possible alternative would be to affirm that sin itself is not sinful.

It is because the natural man loves sin and hates God that he has no inclination and will to keep His law. But far from excusing him, that constitutes the very essence of his guilt. We are told that Joseph's brothers "hated him, and could not speak peaceably unto him" (Gen. 37:4). Why was it that they were unable to speak peaceably to him? Not because they lacked vocal organs, but because they hated him so much. Was such inability excusable? No, in that consisted the greatness of their guilt. An apostle makes mention of men "having eyes full of adultery, and that cannot cease from sin" (2 Pet. 2:14). But was not their impotence culpable? Surely it was; the reason they could not cease from sin was that their eyes were "full of adultery." Far from such an inability being an innocent one, it constituted the enormity of their crime; far from excusing them, it made their sin greater. Men must indeed be blind when they fail to see it is their moral impotence, their voluntary slavery to sin, which makes them obnoxious in the sight of the holy One.

A man's heart being fully set in him to do evil does not render his sinful actions the less criminal, but the more so. Consider the opposite: Does the strength of a virtuous disposition render a good action less or more praiseworthy? God is no less glorious because He is so infinitely and unchangeably holy in His nature that He "cannot be tempted with evil" (Jam. 1:13) nor act otherwise than in the most righteous and perfect manner. Holiness constitutes the very excellence of the divine character. Is Satan any less sinful and criminal because he is of such a devilish disposition, so full of unreasonable malice against God and men, as to be incapable of anything but the most horrible wickedness? So of humanity. No one supposes that the want of a will to work excuses a man from work, as physical incapacity does. No one imagines that the covetous miser, with his useless hoard of gold, with no heart to give a penny to the poor, is for that reason excused from deeds of charity as though he had nothing to give.

God's Just Rights

How justly, then, may God still enforce His rights and demand loyal allegiance from men. God will not relinquish His claims because the creature has sinned nor lower His requirements because he has ruined himself. Were God to command that which we ardently desired and truly endeavored to do, but for which we lacked the requisite faculties, we should not be to blame. But when He commands us to love Him with all our hearts and we refuse to do so, we are most certainly to blame, notwithstanding our moral impotence, because we still possess the necessary faculties for the exercise of such love. This is precisely what sin consists of: the want of affection for God with its suitable expression in obedient acts, the presence of an inveterate enmity against Him with its works of disobedience. Were God to grant rebels against His government the license to freely indulge their evil proclivities, that would be to abandon the platform of His holiness and to condone if not endorse their wickedness.

William Cunningham said:

There is no difficulty in seeing the reasons why God might address such commands to fallen and depraved men. The moral law is a transcript of God's moral perfections, and must ever continue unchangeable. It must always be binding, in all its extent, upon all rational and responsible creatures, from the very condition of their existence, from their necessary relation to God. It constitutes the only accurate representation of the duty universally and at all times incumbent upon rational beings,—the duty which God must of necessity impose upon and require of them. Man was able to obey this law, to discharge this whole duty, in the condition in which he was created. If he is now in a different condition—one in which he is no longer able to discharge this duty—this does not remove or invalidate his obligation to perform it; it does not affect the reasonableness and propriety of God, on the ground of His own perfections, and of the relation in which He stands to His creatures, proclaiming and imposing this obligation—requiring of men to do what is still as much as ever incumbent upon them.

It has generally been lost sight of that the moral law is not only the rule of our works but also of our strength. Inasmuch as well-being is the ground of well doing—the tree must be good before the fruit can be—we are obliged to conclude that the law is the rule of our nature as truly as it is of our deeds. "Thou shalt love the Lord thy God with all thine heart, and with all thy soul, and with all thy might" (Deut. 6:5). That was said not only to unfallen Adam but also to his fallen descendants. The Savior repeated it: "Thou shalt love the Lord thy God with all thy heart, and with all thy soul, and with all thy strength" (Luke 10:27). The law not only requires us to love, but to have minds equipped with all strength to love God, so that there may be life and vigor in our love and obedience to Him. The law requires no more love than it does strength; if it did not require strength to love, it would require no love either. Thus it is plain that God not only enforces His rightful demands upon fallen man, but also has not abated one iota of His requirements because of the fall.

If the divine law said nothing more to the natural man today than "Thou shalt love the Lord thy God with what strength thou now hast"—rather than with the strength He requires him to have and which He first gave to him, so that both strength and faculty, love and its manifestation, came under the command—it would amount to "Thou needest not love the Lord thy God at all, for thou art now without strength and therefore incapable of loving and serving Him, and art not to be blamed for having none." But as we have shown, man is culpable for his impotence. The only reason why he does not love God is because his heart holds enmity against Him. Did a murderer ever plead at the bar of justice that he hated his victim so intensely that he could not go near him without killing him? If such were his acknowledgment, it would only aggravate his crime; he would stand condemned by his own word. Hell, then, must be the only final place for inalienable rebels against God.

We should also call attention to the propriety of the divine law being pressed upon fallen man, in all the length and breadth of its requirements, both as a means of knowledge and a means of conviction, even though no longer available as a standard which he is able to measure up to. In spite of man's inability to obey it, the law serves to inform him of the holy character of God, the relation in which he stands to Him, and the duty which He still requires of him. Also it serves as an essential means of convicting men of their depravity. Since they are sinners, it is most important that they should be made aware of the fact. If their duty is made clear, if they are told to do that which is incumbent upon them, they are more likely to perceive how far short they come. If they are stirred up to compliance with God's requirements, to a discharge of their obligations, they will discover their moral helplessness in a way more forcible than any sermons can convey.

In the next place let us point out that fallen man is responsible to use means both for the avoidance of sin and the performance of holiness. Though the unregenerate are destitute of spiritual life, they are not therefore mere machines. The natural man has a rational faculty and a moral sense which distinguish between right and wrong, and he is called upon to exert those faculties. Far from being under an inevitable necessity of living in known and gross sins, it is only because of deliberate perversity that any do so. The most profane swearer is able to refrain from his oaths when in the presence of someone whom he fears and to whom he knows it would be displeasing. Let a drunkard see poison put into his liquor, and it would stand by him untasted from morning until night. Criminals are deterred from many offenses by the sight of a policeman, though they have no fear of God in their hearts. Thus self-control is not utterly outside man's power.

"Enter not into the path of the wicked, and go not in the way of evil men. Avoid it, pass not by it, turn from it, and pass away" (Prov. 4:14-

15). Is not the natural man capable of heeding such warnings? It is the duty of the sinner to shun everything which has a tendency to lead to wrongdoing, to turn his back on every approach to evil and every custom which leads to wickedness. If we deliberately play with fire and are burned, the blame rests wholly on ourselves. There is still in the nature of fallen man some power to resist temptation, and the more it is asserted the stronger it becomes; otherwise there would be no more sin in yielding to an evil solicitation than there is sin in a tree being blown down by a hurricane. Moreover, God does not deny grace to those who humbly and earnestly seek it from Him in His appointed ways. When men are influenced to passion, to allurements, to vice, they are blamable and must justly give account to God.

No rational creature acts without some motive. The planets move as they are driven, and if a counter-influence supervenes, they have no choice but to leave their course and follow it. But man has a power of resistance which they do not have, and he may strengthen by indulgence or weaken by resistance the motives which induce him to commit wrong. How often we hear of athletes voluntarily submitting to the most rigorous discipline and self-denial; does not that evince that the natural man has power to refrain from self-indulgence when he is pleased to use it. Highly paid vocalists, abstaining from all forms of intemperance in order to keep themselves physically fit, illustrate the same principle. Abimelech, a heathen king, took Sarah for himself; but when God warned him that she was another man's wife, he did not touch her. Observe carefully what the Lord said to him: "I know that thou didst this in the integrity of thine heart; for I also withheld thee from sinning against me: therefore suffered I thee not to touch her" (Gen. 20:6). Abimelech had a natural "integrity" which God acknowledged to be in him, though He also affirmed His own power in restraining him. If men would nourish their integrity, God would concur with them to preserve them from many sins.

Not only is man responsible to use means for the avoidance of evil, but he is under binding obligation to employ the appointed means for the furtherance of good. It is true that the efficacy of means lies in the sovereign power of God and not in the industry of man; nevertheless He has established a definite connection between the means and the end desired. God has appointed that bodily life shall be sustained by bodily food, and if a man deliberately starves himself to death he is guilty of self-destruction. Men still have power to utilize the outward means, the principal ones of which are hearing the Word and practicing prayer. They have the same feet to take them to church as conduct them to the theater, the same ability to pray to God as the heathen have to cry to idols. Slothfulness will be reproved in the day of judgment (Matt. 25:26). The sinner's plea that he had no heart for these duties will mean nothing. He will have to answer for his contempt of God.

Because he is a rational creature, man has the power to exercise consideration. He does so about many things; why not about his soul? God

Himself testifies to this power even in a sinful nation. To His prophet He said, "Thou shalt remove from thy place to another place in their sight: it may be they will consider, though they be a rebellious house" (Ezek. 12:3). Christ condemned men for their failure at this very point: "Ye hypocrites, ye can discern the face of the sky and of the earth; but how is it that ye do not discern this time? Yea, and why even of yourselves judge ye not what is right?" (Luke 12:56-57). If men have the ability to take an inventory of their business, why not of their eternal concerns'? Refusal to do so is criminal negligence. "All the ends of the world shall remember and turn unto the Lord" (Ps. 22:27). The natural man possesses the faculty of memory and is obligated to put it to the best use. "Let us search and try our ways, and turn again to the Lord" (Lam. 3:40). Failure to do so is willful negligence.

Man has not only physical organs but affections, or passions. If Esau could weep for the loss of his blessing, why not for his sins? Observe the charge which God brought against Ephraim: "They will not frame their doings to turn unto their God" (Hosea 5:4). They would entertain no thoughts nor perform any actions that had the least prospect toward reformation. The unregenerate are capable of considering their ways. They know they shall not continue in this life forever, and most of them are persuaded in their conscience that after death there is an appointed judgment. True, the sinner cannot save himself, but he can obstruct his own mercies. Not only do men refuse to employ the means which God has appointed but they scorn His help by fighting against illumination and conviction. Remember Joseph's brothers: "We are verily guilty concerning our brother, in that we saw the anguish of his soul, when he besought us, and we would not hear" (Gen. 42:21). "Ye do always resist the Holy Ghost" (Acts 7:51).

Summary of Man's Liability to God

How can the natural man be held responsible to glorify God when he is incapable of doing so? Let us summarize our answers. First, sin has not produced any change in the essential relation between the creature and the Creator; nothing can alter God's right to command and to be obeyed. Second, sin has not taken away the moral agency of man, consequently he is as much a subject of God's moral government as he ever was. Third, since man still possesses faculties which are suited to the substance of God's commands, he is under binding obligations to serve his Maker. Fourth, the moral inability of man is not brought about by any external compulsion, for nothing outside of man can impose upon him any necessity of sinning; because all sin issues out of his own heart, he must be held accountable for it. Fifth, man's servitude to sin was self-induced and is self-perpetuated, and since he freely chooses to do evil he is inexcusable. Sixth, man's inability is moral and not constitutional, consisting of enmity against and opposition to God; therefore it is punishable. Seventh, because man refuses to use those means which are suited to lead to his recovery and scorns the help which is proffered him, he deliberately destroys himself.

It should be pointed out that, in spite of all the excuses offered by the sinner in defense of his moral impotence, in spite of the outcries he makes against the justice of being required to render to God that which lies altogether beyond his power, the sentence of his condemnation is articulated within his own being. Man's very consciousness testifies to his responsibility, and his conscience witnesses to the criminality of his wrongdoing. The common language of man under the lashings of conscience is "I might have done otherwise; O what a fool I have been! I was faithfully warned by those who sought my good, but I was self-willed. I had convictions against wrongdoing, but I stifled them. My present wretchedness is the result of my own madness. No one is to blame but myself." The very fact that men universally blame themselves for their folly establishes their accountability and evinces their guilt.

If we are to attain anything approaching completeness of this aspect of our subject it is necessary to consider the particular and special case of the Christian's inability. This is a real yet distinct branch of our theme, though all the writers we have consulted appear to have studiously avoided it. This is in some respects admittedly the most difficult part of our problem, yet that is no reason why it should be evaded. If Holy Writ has nothing to say on the subject, then we must be silent too; but if it makes pronouncement, it is our duty to believe and try to understand what that pronouncement signifies. As we have seen, the Word of God plainly and positively affirms the moral impotence of the natural man to do good, yet at the same time teaches throughout that his depravity does not supply the slightest extenuation for his transgression against the divine law. But the question we now desire to look squarely in the face is How is it with the one who has been born again? Wherein does his case and condition differ from what it was previously, both with respect to his ability to do those things which are pleasing to God and with respect to the extent of his responsibility?

Are we justified in employing the expression "the Christian's spiritual impotence?" Is it not a contradiction in terms? Scripture does warrant the use of it. "Without me ye can do nothing" (John 15:5) connotes that the believer has no power of his own to bring forth any fruit to the glory of God. "For to will is present with me; but how to perform that which is good I find not" (Rom. 7:18). Such an acknowledgment from the most eminent of the apostles makes it plain that no saint has strength of his own to meet the divine requirements. "Not that we are sufficient of ourselves to think any thing as of ourselves" (2 Cor. 3:5). If insufficient of ourselves to even think a good thought, how much less can we perform a good deed. "For the flesh lusteth against the Spirit, and the Spirit against the flesh: and these are contrary the one to the other: so that ye cannot do the things that ye would" (Gal. 5:17). That "cannot" clearly authorizes us to speak of the Christian's inability. Every prayer for divine succor and strength is a tacit confirmation of the same truth.

Then if such be the case of the Christian, is he in this regard any better off than the non-Christian? Does not this evacuate regeneration of its miraculous and most blessed element? We must indeed be careful not to disparage the gracious work of the Spirit in the new birth, nevertheless we must not lose sight of the fact that regeneration is only the beginning of His good work in the elect (Phil. 1:6), the best of whom are but imperfectly sanctified in this life (Phil. 3:12). That there is a real, radical difference between the unregenerate and the regenerate is gloriously true. The former are dead in trespasses and sins; the latter have passed from death to life. The former are the subjects and slaves of the devil; the latter have been delivered from the power of darkness and translated into the kingdom of God's dear Son (Col. 1:13). The former are completely and helplessly under the dominion of sin; the latter have been made free from sin's dominion and have become the servants of righteousness (Rom. 6:14, 18). The former despise and reject Christ; the latter love and desire to serve Him.

In seeking to grapple with the problem of the Christian's spiritual inability and the nature and extent of his responsibility, there are two dangers to be avoided, two extremes to guard against: (1) practically reducing the Christian to the level of the unregenerate, which is virtually a denial of the reality and blessedness of regeneration; (2) making out the Christian to be very nearly independent and self-sufficient. We must aim at preserving the balance between "Without me ye can do nothing" (John 15:5) and "I can do all things through Christ which strengtheneth me" (Phil. 4:13). What we are now discussing is part of the Christian paradox, for the believer is often a mystery to himself and a puzzle to others because of the strange and perplexing contrarieties meeting in him. He is the Lord's free man, yet declares, "I am carnal, sold under sin" (Rom. 7:14). He rejoices in the law of the Lord, yet cries, "O wretched man that I am!" (Rom. 7:24). He acknowledges to the Lord "I believe," yet in the same breath prays, "Help Thou my unbelief." He declares, "When I am weak then am I strong." One moment he is praising his Savior and the next groaning before Him.

Wherein does the regenerate differ from the unregenerate? First, the regenerate has been given an understanding that he may know Him who is true (1 John 5:20). His mind has been supernaturally illumined; the spiritual light which shines in his heart (2 Cor. 4:6) capacitates him to discern spiritual things in a spiritual and transforming manner (2 Cor. 3:18); nevertheless its development may be hindered by neglect and sloth. Second, the regenerate has a liberated will, so that he is capacitated to consent to and embrace spiritual things. His will has been freed from that total bondage and dominion of sin under which he lay by nature; nevertheless he is still dependent upon God's working in him both to will and to do of His good pleasure. Third, his affections are changed so that he is capacitated to relish and delight in the things of God; therefore he exclaims, "O how love I Thy law." Before, he saw no beauty in Christ, but now He is "altogether lovely." Sin which was formerly a spring of pleasure is now a fountain of sorrow. Fourth, his conscience is renewed, so that it reproves him for sins of which he was not previously aware and discloses corruptions which he never suspected.

But if on the one hand there is a radical difference between the regenerate and the unregenerate, it is equally true that there is a vast difference between the Christian in this life and the Christian in the life to come. While we must be careful not to belittle the Spirit's work in regeneration, we must be equally on our guard lest we lose sight of the believer's entire dependence on God. Although a new nature is imparted at regeneration, the believer is still a creature (2 Cor. 5:17); the new nature is not to be looked to, rested in or made an idol. Though the believer has had the principle of grace communicated to him, yet he has no store of grace within himself from which he may now draw. He is but a "babe" (1 Pet. 2:2), completely dependent on Another for everything. The new nature does not of itself empower or enable the soul for a life of obedience and the performance of duty; it simply fits and makes it compatible to these. The principle of spiritual life requires its Bestower to call it into operation. The believer is, in that respect, like a becalmed ship—waiting for a heavenly breeze to set it in motion.

Yet in another sense the believer resembles the crew of the ship rather than the vessel itself, and in this he differs from those who are unrenewed. Before regeneration we are wholly passive, incapable of any cooperation; but after regeneration we have a renewed mind to judge aright and a will to choose the things of God when moved by Him; nevertheless we are dependent on His moving us. We are daily dependent on God's strengthening, exciting and directing the new nature, so that we need to pray "Incline my heart unto thy testimonies . . . and quicken thou me in thy way" (Ps. 119:36-37). The new birth is a vastly different thing from the winding of a clock so that it will run of itself; rather the strongest believer is like a glass without a base, which cannot stand one moment longer than it is held. The believer has to wait upon the Lord for his strength to be renewed (Isa. 40:31). The Christian's strength is sustained solely by the constant operations and communications of the Holy Spirit, and he lives spiritually only as he clings close to Christ and draws virtue from Him.

There is a suitableness or answerableness between the new nature and the requirements of God so that His commands "are not grievous" to it (1 John 5:3), so that Wisdom's ways are found to be "pleasant" and all her paths "peace" (Prov. 3:17). Nevertheless the believer stands in constant need of the help of the Spirit, working in him both to will and to do, granting fresh supplies of grace to enable him to perform his spiritual desires. A simple delight in the divine law is not of itself sufficient to produce obedience. We have to pray, "Make me to go in the path of thy commandments" (Ps. 119:35). Regeneration conveys to us an inclination and tendency for that which is good, thereby fitting us for the Master's use; nevertheless we have to look outside ourselves for enabling grace: "Be strong in the grace that is in Christ Jesus" (2 Tim. 2:1). Thereby God removes all ground for boasting. He would have all the glory given to His grace: "By the grace of God I am what I am" (1 Cor. 15:10).

If enough rain fell in one day to suffice for several years we would not so clearly discern the mercies of God in His providence nor be kept looking to Him for continued supplies. So it is in connection with our spiritual lives: we are daily made to feel that "our sufficiency is of God." The believer is entirely dependent on God for the exercise of his faith and for the right use of his knowledge. Said the apostle: "I live; yet not I, but Christ liveth in me" (Gal. 2:20), which gives the true emphasis and places the glory where it belongs. But he at once added, "And the life which I now live in the flesh I live by the faith of the Son of God [by the faith of which He is its Object], who loved me, and gave himself for me." That preserves the true balance. Though it was Christ who lived in and empowered him, yet he was not passive and idle. He put forth acts of faith in Him and thereby drew virtue from Him; thus he could do all things through Christ strengthening him.

Responsibility of the Christian

It is at that very point the responsibility of the Christian appears. As a creature his responsibility is the same as pertains to the unregenerate, but as a new creature in Christ Jesus (2 Cor. 5:17) he has incurred increased obligations: "Unto whomsoever much is given, of him shall be much required" (Luke 12:48). The Christian is responsible to walk in newness of life, to bring forth fruit for God as one who is alive from the dead, to grow in grace and in the knowledge of the Lord, to use his spiritual endowments and to improve or employ his talents. The call comes to him "Stir up the gift of God, which is in thee" (2 Tim. 1:6). Isaiah the prophet complained of God's people, "There is none that stirreth up himself to lay hold of thee" (64:7), which condemns slothfulness and spiritual lethargy. The Christian is responsible to use all the means of grace which God has provided for his wellbeing, looking to Him for His blessing upon them. When the Scripture says, "The Spirit also helpeth our infirmities" (Rom. 8:26), the Greek verb is "helpeth together"—He cooperates with our diligence not our idleness.

The Christian has received spiritual life, and all life is a power to act by. Inasmuch as that spiritual life is a principle of grace animating all the faculties of the soul, he is capacitated to use all means of grace which God has provided for his growth and to avoid everything which would hinder or retard his growth. He is required to keep the heart with all diligence (Prov. 4:23), for if the fountain is kept clean, the springs which issue from it will be pure. He is required to "make not provision for the flesh, to fulfill the lusts thereof" (Rom. 13:14), not allowing his mind and affections to fix themselves on sinful or unlawful objects. He is required to deny himself, take up his cross and follow the example which Christ has left him. He is commanded to "love not the world, neither the things that are in the world" (1 John 2:15), and therefore he must conduct himself as a stranger and pilgrim in this scene of action, abstaining from fleshly lusts which war against the soul (1 Pet. 2:11) if he would not lose the heavenly inheritance (1 Cor. 9:27). And for the performance of these difficult duties he must diligently and earnestly seek supplies of grace counting on God to bless the means to him.

No small part of the Christian's burden and grief is the inward opposition he meets, thwarting his aspirations and bringing him into captivity to that which he hates. The believer's "life" is a hidden one (Col. 3:3), and so also is his conflict. He longs to love and serve God with all his heart and to be holy in every detail of his life, but the flesh resists the spirit. Worldliness, unbelief, coldness, slothfulness exert their power. The believer struggles against their influence and groans under their bondage. He desires to be clothed with humility, but pride is constantly breaking forth in some form or other. He finds that he cannot attain to that which he desires and approves. He discovers a wide disparity between what he knows and does, between what he believes and practices, between his aims and realizations. Truly he is "an unprofitable servant." He is so often defeated in the conflict that he is frequently faint and weary in the use of means and in performance of duty; he may question the genuineness of his profession and be tempted to give up the fight.

In seeking to help distressed saints concerning this acute problem, the servant of God needs to be very careful lest he foster a false peace in those who have a historical faith in the gospel but are total strangers to its saving power. God's servant must be especially watchful not to bolster the false hopes of those who delight in the mercy of God but hate His holiness, who misappropriate the doctrine of His grace and make it subservient to their lusts. He must therefore call upon his hearers to honestly and diligently examine themselves before God, that they may discover whence the inward oppositions arise and what are their reactions to them. They must determine whether these inconsistencies spring from an unwillingness to wear the yoke of Christ, their whole hearts accompanying and consenting to such resistances to God's righteous requirements, or whether these oppositions to God's laws have their rise in corruptions which they sincerely endeavor to oppose, which they hate, which they mourn over, which they confess to God and long to be released from.

When describing the conflict in himself between the flesh and the spirit— between indwelling sin and the principle of grace he had received at the new birth—the Apostle Paul declared, "For that which I do [which is contrary to the holy requirements of God] I allow not [I do not approve of it; it is foreign to my real inclinations and purpose of heart]: but what I hate, that do I" (Rom. 7:15). Paul detested and yearned to be delivered from the evil which rose up within him. Far from affording him any satisfaction, it was his great burden and grief. And thus it is with every truly regenerated soul when he is in his right mind. He may be, yes is, frequently overcome by his carnal and worldly lusts; but instead of being pleased at such experience and contentedly lying down in his sins, as a sow delights to wallow in the mire, he cries in distress, confesses such failures as grievous sins, and prays to be cleansed from them.

"If I were truly regenerate, how could sin rage so fiercely within and so often obtain the mastery over me?" This question deeply exercises many of God's people. Yet the Scripture declares, "A just man falleth seven times" (Prov. 24:16); but it at once adds "and riseth up again." Did not David lament, "Iniquities prevail against me" (Ps. 65:3)? Yet if you are striving to mortify your lusts, looking daily to the blood of Christ to pardon, and begging the Spirit to more perfectly sanctify you, you may add with the psalmist, "As for our transgressions, thou shalt purge them away." Indeed, did not the highly favored apostle declare, "For we know that the law is spiritual: but I am carnal, sold [not 'unto' but] under sin" (Rom. 7:14). There is a vast difference between Paul and Ahab, of whom we read that he "did sell himself to work wickedness in the sight of the Lord" (I Kings 21:25). It is the difference between one who is taken captive in war, becoming a slave unwillingly and longing for deliverance, and one who voluntarily abandons himself to a course of open defiance of the Almighty and who so loves evil that he would refuse release.

We must distinguish between sin's dominion over the unregenerate and sin s tyranny and usurpation over the regenerate. Dominion follows upon right of conquest or subjection. Sin's great design in all of us is to obtain undisputed dominion; it has it in unbelievers and contends for it in believers. But every evidence the Christian has that he is under the rule of grace is that much evidence he is not under the dominion of sin. "For I delight in the law of God after the inward man: But I see another law in my members, warring against the law of my mind, and bringing me into captivity to the law of sin which is in my members" (Rom. 7:22-23). That does not mean that sin always triumphs in the act, but that it is a hostile power which the renewed soul cannot evict. It wars against us in spite of all we can do. The general makeup of believers is that, notwithstanding sin being a "law" (governing force) not "to" but "in" them, they "would [desire and resolve to] do good," but "evil is present" with them. Their habitual inclination is to good, and they are brought into captivity against their will. It is the "flesh" which prevents the full realization of their holy aspirations in this life.

But if the Son has "made us free" (John 8:36), how can Christians be in bondage? The answer is that Christ has already freed them from the guilt and penalty, love and dominion of sin, but not yet from its presence. As the believer hungers and thirsts after righteousness, pants for communion with the living God, and yearns to be perfectly conformed to the image of Christ, he is "free from sin"; but as such longings are more or less thwarted by indwelling corruptions, he is still "sold under sin." Then let prevailing lusts humble you, cause you to be more watchful and to look more diligently to Christ for deliverance; then those very exercises will evidence a principle of grace in you which desires and seeks after the destruction of inborn sin. Those who have hearts set on pleasing God are earnest in seeking enabling grace from Him, yet they must remember He works in them both to will and to do of His good pleasure, maintaining His sovereignty in this as in everything else. Bear in mind that it is allowed sin which paralyzes the new nature.

Thus God has not yet uprooted sin from the soul of the believer, but allows him to groan under its uprisings, that his pride may be stained and his heart made to constantly feel he is not worthy of the least of God's mercies. To produce in him that feeling of dependence on divine power and grace. To exalt the infinite condescension and patience of God in the apprehension of the humbled saint. To place the crown of glory on the only head worthy to wear it: "Not unto us, O Lord, not unto us, but unto thy name give glory, for thy mercy, and for thy truth's sake" (Ps. 115:1).

Chapter 10
Opposition

In bringing this study to a close it seems desirable that we should consider the opposition made against this truth before giving an exposition of it. This subject of the moral inability of fallen man for good is peculiarly repugnant to his pride, and therefore it is not surprising that his outcry against it is so loud and prolonged. The exposure of human depravity, the disclosure of the fearful ruin which sin has wrought in our constitution, cannot be a pleasant thing to contemplate and still less to acknowledge as a fact. To heartily own that by nature I am devoid of love for God, that I am full of inveterate enmity against Him, is diametrically opposed to my whole makeup. It is only natural to form a high estimate of ourselves and to entertain exalted views of both our capabilities and our good intentions. To be assured on divine authority that our hearts are incurably wicked, that we love darkness rather than light, that we hate alike the law and the gospel, is revolting to our whole being. Every possible effort is put forth by the carnal mind to repudiate such a flesh-withering and humiliating description of human nature. If it cannot be refuted by an appeal to facts, then it must be held up to ridicule.

Man's Refusal to Accept the Doctrine
Such opposition to the truth should neither surprise nor discourage us, for it has been plainly announced to us: "The natural man receiveth not the things of the Spirit of God: for they are foolishness unto him" (1 Cor. 2:14). The very fact that they are foolishness to him should lead us to expect he will laugh at and scorn them. Nor must we be alarmed when we find this mocking of the truth is far from being confined to avowed infidels and open enemies of God; this same antagonism appears in the great majority of religious persons and those who pose as the champions of Christianity. Passing through a seminary and putting on the ministerial garb does not transform the unregenerate into regenerate men. When our Lord announced, "The truth shall make you free," it was the religious leaders of the Jews who declared they were never in bondage; and when He affirmed, "Ye are of your father the devil, and the lusts of your father ye will do," they replied, "Say we not well that thou art a Samaritan, and hast a devil?" (John 8).

Principal Objections
It is just because the fiercest opposition to this truth comes from those

inside Christendom, not from those outside, that we consider it wise to face the principal objections. We do so to place the Lord's people on their guard and to let them see there is no weight in such criticism. We would not waste time in seeking to close the mouths of those whom God Himself will deal with in due time, but we desire to expose their sophistries so that those with spiritual discernment may perceive that their faith rests on a foundation which no outbursts of unbelief can shake. Every objection against the doctrine of man's spiritual impotence has been overthrown by God's servants in the past, yet each fresh generation repeats the arrogance of its forebears. We have already refuted most of these objections in the course of this study, yet by now assembling them together and showing their pointlessness we may render a service which will not be entirely useless.

1. If fallen man is unable to keep God's law, he cannot be obligated to keep it. Impotence obviously cancels responsibility. A child three or four years of age ought not to be whipped because it does not read and write. A legless man should not be sent to prison because he does not walk. Surely a just and holy God does not require sinful creatures to render perfect obedience to a divine and spiritual law.

How is this objection to be met? First, by pointing out that it is not based upon Holy Writ but is merely human reasoning. Scripture affirms again and again that fallen man is spiritually impotent, "without strength," and that he "cannot please God"; from that nothing must move us. Scripture nowhere states that spiritual helplessness releases man from God's claims upon him; therefore no human reasoning to the contrary, however plausible or pleasing, is entitled to any consideration from those who tremble at God's Word. Scripture reveals that God does hold fallen man responsible to keep His law, for He gave it to Israel at Sinai and pronounced His curse upon all transgressors of it.

What has been pointed out should be sufficient for any simple soul who fears the Lord. But lest it be thought that this is all which can be said by way of refutation, lest it be supposed that this objection is so forceful that it cannot be met in a more direct rebuttal, we add the following: To declare that man cannot be obligated to keep the law if he is unable to do so demands an inquiry into both the nature and the cause of his inability. Once that investigation is entered into, the sophistry of the objection will quickly appear. Wherein lies man's inability to keep God's law? Is it the absence of the requisite faculties or his unwillingness to use aright the faculties with which he is endowed? Were fallen man devoid of reason, conscience, will, there would be some force in this objection; but since he is possessed of all those faculties which constitute a moral being, it is quite inane and invalid. There is no analogy whatever between the sinner's inability to travel the highway of holiness and the inability of a legless man to walk.

The worthlessness of this objection is made evident not only when we examine the nature of man's spiritual impotence; it equally appears void when we diagnose its cause. Why is fallen man unable to keep God's law? Is it because he is worked upon by some almighty being who prevents him from rendering obedience? Were fallen man truly desirous of serving and pleasing God, were it a case of his ardently longing to do so but being thwarted because another more powerful than himself hindered him, there would be some force to this objection. But God, far from placing any obstacle in our way, sets before us every conceivable inducement to comply with His precepts. If it be argued that the devil is more powerful than man and that he is continually seeking to turn him from the path of rectitude, the answer is that Satan can do nothing without our own consent. All he can do is to tempt to wrongdoing; it is man's own will which either yields or refuses.

In reply to what has last been pointed out, someone may say, "But fallen man has no sufficient power of his own with which to successfully resist Satan's evil solicitations." Suppose that be so, then what? Does that oblige us to take sides with the enemies of the truth and affirm that therefore man is to be excused for his sinful deeds, that he is not obligated to render perfect obedience to the law merely because he does not have the power to cope with his adversary? Not at all. Once more we must inquire as to the cause. Why is it that man cannot put the devil to flight? Is it because he was originally vested with less moral strength than his foe possesses? No indeed, for he was made in the image and likeness of God. Man's present inability has been brought about by an act of his own and not by any stinginess or oversight of his Creator. "Thou hast destroyed thyself" (Hosea 13:9) is the divine verdict. Though man is unable to recover what he lost, he has none but himself to blame for his willful and wicked destruction of his original strength.

It is at this very point man twists and wriggles most, seeking to get from under the onus which righteously rests on him. When Adam offended against the divine law he sought to throw the blame upon his wife, and she in turn upon the devil; ever since then the great majority have attempted to cast it on God Himself, on the pretext that He is the One who gave them being and sent them into the world in their present handicapped condition. It must be kept steadily in mind that original ability destroyed by self-determination does not and cannot destroy the original obligation any more than weakened moral strength by self-indulgence and the formation of evil habits destroys or diminishes obligation. To say otherwise would be to declare that the result of sin excuses sin itself, which is a manifest absurdity. Man's wrongdoing certainly does not annul God's rights. God is no Egyptian taskmaster .requiring men to make bricks without straw. He endowed man with everything requisite for the discharge of his duty, and though man has squandered his substance in riotous living, that does not free him from God's just claims upon him.

The drunkard is certainly less able to obey the law of temperance than the sober man is, yet that law has precisely the same claims upon the former as it has upon the latter. In commercial life the loss of ability to pay does not release from obligation; the loss of property does not free man from his indebtedness. A man is as much a debtor to his creditors after his bankruptcy as he was previously. It is a legal maxim that bankruptcy does not invalidate contracts. Someone may point out that an insolvent debtor cannot be sued in the courts. Nevertheless, even if human law declares it equitable to free an insolvent debtor, the law of God does not. And that verdict is righteous, for the sinner's inability to give God His due is voluntary—he does not wish to pay because he hates Him. Thus both the nature and the cause of man's inability demonstrate that he is "without excuse."

2. When inquiry is made as to the cause of man's spiritual impotence and when it has been shown that this lies not in the Creator but in man's own original rebellion, the objector, far from being silenced, will demur against his being penalized for what his first parents did. He may ask, "Is it just that I should be sent into this world in a state of spiritual helplessness because of their offense? I did not make myself; if I was created with a corrupt nature, why should I be held to blame for its inevitable fruits?" First, let it be pointed out that it is not essential in order for a fallen creature to be blamable for his evil dispositions and acts that he must first be inherently holy. A person who is depraved, who from his heart hates God and despises His law, is nonetheless a sinner because he has been depraved from his birth. His having sinned from the beginning and throughout his existence is surely no valid excuse for his sinning now. Nor is his guilt any the less because his depravity is so deeply rooted in his nature. The stronger his enmity against God the greater its heinousness.

But how can man be condemned for his evil heart when Adam corrupted human nature? Fallen man is voluntarily an enemy to the infinitely glorious God and nothing can extenuate such vile hostility. The very fact that in the day of judgment "every mouth will be stopped" (Rom. 3:19) demonstrates there can be no force in this objection. It is the free and self-determined acting out of his nature for which the sinner will be held accountable. The fact that we are born traitors to God cannot cancel our obligation to give Him allegiance. None can escape the righteous requirements of the law by deliberate opposition to it. That man's nature is the direct consequence of Adam's transgression does not to the slightest degree mitigate his own sins. Is it not a solemn fact that each of us has approved Adam's transgression by following his example and joining with him in rebellion against God? That we go on to break the divine law demonstrates that we are justly condemned with Adam. If we resent our being corrupted through Adam, why not repudiate him and refuse to sin, stand out in opposition to him and be holy?

Yet still the carnal mind will ask, "Since I lost all power to love and serve God even before I was born, how can I be held accountable to do what I cannot? Wherein is the justice in requiring from me what it is impossible to render?" Exactly what was it that man lost by the fall? It was a heart that loved God. And it is the possessing of a heart which has no love for God that is the very essence of human depravity. It is this in which the vileness of fallen man consists: no heart for God. But does a loveless heart for God excuse fallen man? No indeed, for that is the very core of his wickedness and guilt. Men never complain of their lack of power for loving the world. And why are they so thoroughly in love with the world? Is it because the world is more excellent and glorious than God is? Certainly not. It is only because fallen man has a heart which naturally loves the world, but he has no heart with which to love God. The world suits and delights him, but God does not; rather, His very perfections repel him.

Now let us put it plainly and honestly: Can our being devoid of any true love for God free us from our obligation to love Him? Can it to the slightest degree lessen our blame for not loving Him? Is He not infinitely worthy of our affections, our homage, our allegiance? None would argue in any other connection as does the objector here. If a king rules wisely and well, is he not entitled to the honor and loyalty of his subjects? If an employer is merciful and considerate, has he not the right to expect his employees to further his interests and carry out his orders? If I am a kind and dutiful parent, shall I not require the esteem and obedience of my children? If my servant or child has no heart to give what is due, shall I not justly consider him blamable and deserving of punishment? Or shall we reason so insanely that the worse man grows the less he is to blame? "A son honoreth his father, and a servant his master: if then I be a father, where is mine honor? And if I be a master, where is my fear? saith the Lord of hosts" (Mal. 1:6).

3. It is objected that if the sinner is so enslaved by sin that he is impotent to do good, his free agency is denied and he is reduced to a mere machine. This is more a metaphysical question than a practical one, being largely a matter of terms. There is a real sense in which the natural man is in bondage; nevertheless within certain limits he is a free agent, for he acts according to his own inclinations without compulsion. There is much confusion on this subject. Freedom of will is not freedom from action; inaction of the will is no more possible than is inaction of the understanding. Nor is freedom of will a freedom from the internal consequences of voluntary action; the formation of a habit is voluntary, but when formed it cannot be eradicated by volition. Nor is freedom of will a freedom from the restraint and regulation of law; the glorified saints will be completely delivered from sin yet regulated by the divine will. Nor is freedom of will a freedom from bias; Christ acted freely, yet being the holy One He could not sin. The unregenerate act freely, that is, spontaneously, agreeably to their desires; yet being depraved, they can neither will nor do anything which is spiritual.

4. If man is spiritually impotent, all exhortations to the performance of spiritual duties are needless and useless. This objection assumes that God would not address His commands to men unless they were able to

obey them. This idea is most presumptuous, for in it man pretends to be capable of judging the reasons which regulate the divine procedure. Has God no right to press His claims because man has wickedly squandered his power to meet them? The divine commands cover not what we can do, but what we should do; not what we are able to do, but what we ought to do. The divine law is set before us, in all the length and breadth of its holy requirements, as a means of knowledge, revealing to us God's character, the relation in which we stand to Him, and the duty which He justly requires of us. It is also a means of conviction, both of our sin and inability. If men are sinners it is important that they should be made aware of the fact—by setting before them a perfect standard that they may see how far short they come of it. If men are unable to discharge the duties incumbent upon them, it is necessary that they should be made aware of their woeful condition—that they should be made to realize their need of salvation.

5. To teach men they are spiritually impotent is to cut the nerve of all religious endeavor. If man is helpless, what is the use of urging him to strive? Necessity is a sufficient reason to act without further encouragement. A man in the water who is ready to drown will try to save his life, even though he cannot swim and some on the banks tell him it is impossible. Again we would press the divine side. There is a necessity on us whenever there is a command from God. If He requires, it behooves man to use the means and leave the issue with Him. Again, spiritual inability is no excuse for negligence and inertia, because God does not refuse strength to perform His bidding if it is humbly, contritely and trustfully sought. When did He ever deny grace to the sinner who waited upon Him in earnest supplication and in consistent use of the means for procuring it? Is not His Word full of promises to seeking souls? If a man has hands and food is set before him, is it not an idle excuse for him to say he cannot eat because he is not moved from above?

6. If the sinner is spiritually powerless, it is only mocking him to tell him to repent of his sins and believe the gospel. To call on the unregenerate to savingly receive Christ as his Lord and Savior is far from mocking him. Did the Son of God mock the rich young ruler when He told him to sell all that he had and follow Him and then he should have treasure in heaven? Certainly not. Had the ruler no power to sell his possessions? Was it not rather lack of inclination, and for such lack was he not justly blamable? Such a demand served to expose the state of his heart. He loved money more than Christ, earthly things above heavenly. The exhortations, warnings and promises set down in the Word are to be pressed on the ungodly so as to make them more inexcusable, so that they may not say in the day to come that, had they been invited to receive such good things, they would have embraced them; that, had they been admonished for their sins, they would have forsaken them. Their own conscience will convict them, and they will know a prophet of God spoke to them.

7. Finally, it is objected that the doctrine of man's spiritual impotence stifles all hope. To tell a man his condition is irremediable, that he can do nothing whatever to better himself, will drive him to despair. This is precisely what is desired. One principal end which must be kept before the preacher is to shatter the self-sufficiency of his hearer. His business is to undermine the spirit of self-righteousness, to break down self-satisfaction, to sweep away those refuges of lies in which men shelter, to convince them of the utter futility of seeking to win heaven by their own endeavors. His business is to bring before them the exalted claims of God's law and to show how far short we come of it, to expose the wickedness of the human heart, to reveal the ruin which sin has wrought, to bring the sinner face to face with the thrice holy God and to make him realize he is utterly unfit to stand before Him. In a word, the business of God's servant is to make his hearer conscious that unless a miracle of grace is performed in him he is lost forever. Not until the sinner feels that he is helpless and hopeless in himself is he prepared to look outside of himself. Despair opens the door of hope! "Thou hast destroyed thyself, but in me is thine help" (Hosea 13:9).

Chapter 11
Exposition
(Intended chiefly for preachers)

THE PRECEDING CHAPTERS should have made it clear that the subject of the sinner's moral impotence is far more than an academic one, more than a flight into theological metaphysics. Rather is it a truth of divine revelation—a unique one—for it will not be found enunciated in any of the leading religions of antiquity, like Zoroastrianism, Buddhism or Confucianism. Nor do we remember finding any trace of it in the poets and philosophers of early Greece. It is truth which is made prominent in the Scriptures, and therefore must be given a place in the pulpit if it is to declare "all the counsel of God." It is closely bound up with the law and the gospel, the great end of the former being to demonstrate its reality, of the latter to make known the remedy. It is one of the chief battering rams which the Spirit directs against the insensate pride of the human heart, for belief in his own capabilities is the foundation on which man's self-righteousness rests. It is the one doctrine which above all others reveals the catastrophic effects of the fall and shuts up the sinner to the sovereign mercy of God as his only hope.

Generalization Not Sufficient

It is not sufficient for the preacher to generalize and speak of "the ruin which sin has wrought" and affirm that man is "totally depraved"; such expressions convey no adequate concept to the modern mind. It is necessary that he should particularize and show from Holy Writ that "they that are in the flesh cannot please God." His task is to paint fallen human nature in its true colors and not deceive by flattery. The state of the natural man is far, far worse than he has any consciousness of. Though he knows he is not perfect, though in serious moments he is aware that all is not well with him, yet he has no realization whatever that his condition is desperate and irremediable so far as all self-help is concerned. A great many people regard religion as a medicine for the soul, and suppose that if it is taken regularly it will ensure their salvation; that if they do this and that and avoid the other, all will be well in the end. They are totally oblivious to the fact that they are "without strength" and can no more perform spiritual duties than the Ethiopian can change his skin or the leopard his spots.

It is a matter of first importance that the moral inability of fallen man should be understood by all. It concerns both young and old, illiterate and educated; therefore each should have right views on the issue. It is most essential that the unsaved should be made aware not only that they are unable to do what God requires of them, but also why they are unable. They should be told the fact that it is impossible for them to "fulfill all righteousness," but also the cause of this impossibility. Their - self-sufficiency cannot be undermined while they believe they have it in their own power to perform God's commands and to comply with the terms of His gospel. Nevertheless they must not be left with the impression that their impotence is a calamity for which they are not to blame, a deprivation for which they are to be pitied; for they are endowed with faculties suited to respond to law and gospel alike. A mistake concerning either of these truths—man's impotence and man's responsibility—is likely to have a fatal consequence.

On the other hand, as long as men imagine they have it in their own power to perform their whole duty or do all that God requires of them in order for them to obtain pardon and eternal life, they feel at ease and are apt to neglect to diligently apply themselves to the performance of that duty. They are not at all likely to pray in earnest or to watch against sin with any anxiety. They neither see the need of God's working in them "both to will and to do of his good pleasure" nor the necessity of their "working out their own salvation with fear and trembling." To wake men out of this dream of self-sufficiency the Savior has given such alarming declarations as these: "Except a man be born again, he cannot see the kingdom of God" (John 3:3); "No man can come to me, except the Father which hath sent me draw him" (John 6:44). And to cut off effectually from the unregenerate all hope of obtaining mercy on the ground of the supposed acceptableness of anything they have done or can do until created in Christ Jesus unto good works, His apostle declared, "They that are in the flesh cannot please God" (Rom. 8:8).

On the other hand, should the unregenerate be allowed to suppose they are devoid of those faculties which are necessary for knowing God's will and doing those things which are pleasing in His sight, such a delusion is likely to prove equally fatal to them. For in that case how could they ever be convinced of either sin or righteousness: of sin in themselves and of righteousness in God? How could they ever perceive that the ways of the Lord are just and their own unjust? If in fact the natural man had no kind of capacity any more than has the horse or mule to love and serve God, to repent and believe the gospel, then the pressing of such duties upon him would be most unreasonable, nor could their noncompliance be at all criminal. Accordingly we find that after our Lord informed Nicodemus of the necessity of man's being born again before he could "see" or believe to the saving of his soul, He declared that he was "condemned already" for not believing (John 3:18). Then He cleared up the whole matter by saying, "This is the condemnation, that light is come into the world, and men loved darkness rather than light, because their deeds were evil.

For every one that doeth evil hateth the light, neither cometh to the light, lest his deeds should be reproved" (vv. 19-20).

Clear Distinctions Necessary

From these and similar verses well-instructed scholars of the Word of God have been led to draw a sharp distinction between the absence of natural faculties and the lack of moral ability, the latter being the essence of moral depravity. The absence of natural faculties clears one from blame, for one who is physically blind is not blameworthy because he cannot see, nor is an idiot to be condemned because he is devoid of rationality. Moral inability is of a totally different species, for it proceeds from an evil heart, consisting of a culpable failure to use in the right way those talents with which God has endowed us. The unregenerate man who refuses to obtain any knowledge of God through reading His Word is justly chargeable with such neglect; but the saint is not guilty because he fails to arrive at a perfect knowledge of God, for such an attainment lies beyond the reach of his faculties.

Some may object to what has just been pointed out and say that this is a distinction of no consequence; inability is inability; what a man cannot do he cannot do; whether it be owing to a lack of faculties or the absence of a good heart, it comes to the same thing. All this is true so far as the end is concerned, but not so far as the criminality. If an evil disposition were a valid excuse, then all the evil in the world would be excusable. Because sin cannot be holiness, is it the less evil? Because the sinner cannot, at the same time, be a saint, is he no more a sinner? Because an evil-minded man cannot get rid of his evil mind while he has no inclination to do so, is he only to be pitied like one who labors under a misconception? True also, this distinction affords no relief to one who is dead in sin, nor does it inform him how he can by his own effort become alive to God; nevertheless, it adds to his condemnation and makes him aware of his awful state.

For vindicating the justice of God, for magnifying His grace, for laying low the haughtiness of man, moral inability is a distinction of vital consequence, however hateful it may be to the ungodly. Unless the line is drawn between excusing a wicked heart and pitying a palsied hand, between moral depravity and the lack of moral faculties, the whole Word of God and all His ways with man must appear invalid, shrouded in midnight darkness. Deny this distinction, and God's requiring perfect obedience from such imperfect creatures must seem altogether unreasonable, His condemning to everlasting misery everyone who does evil (when doing evil is what no man can avoid) excessively harsh. But let men be made aware of the horrible plague of their hearts, let the distinct difference between the absence of moral faculties and the sinful misuse of them be seen and felt, and every mouth will be stopped and all the world become guilty before God.

Though at first it may seem to the preacher that the proclamation of human impotence defeats his ends and works against the highest interest of his hearers, yet if God is pleased to bless his fidelity to the truth (and faith may always count upon such blessing), it will do the hearer good in his latter end, for it will drive him out from the hiding place of falsehood, it will bring him to realize his need of fleeing for refuge to the glorious hope set before him in the gospel. By pulling down strongholds, casting down imaginations and every high thing that exalts itself against God, the way is paved for bringing into captivity every thought to the obedience of Christ. To see oneself "without strength" and at the same time "without excuse" is indeed humiliating, yet this must be seen by the sinner—before either the justice of the divine law or one's utter helplessness and conviction of guilt—as the chief prerequisite for embracing Christ as one's all-sufficient Savior.

It will thus be seen that there are two chief dangers concerning which the preacher must be on his guard while endeavoring to expound this doctrine. First, while pressing the utter inability of the natural man to meet the just claims of God or even so much as perform a single spiritual duty, he must not overthrow or even weaken the equally evident fact of man's moral responsibility. Second, in his zeal to leave unimpaired the moral agency and personal accountability of the sinner, he must not repudiate his total depravity and death in trespasses and sins. This is no easy task, and here as everywhere the minister is made to feel his need of seeking wisdom from above. Yet let it be pointed out that prayer is not designed as a substitute for hard work and study, but rather as a preparative for the same. Difficulties are not to be shunned, but overcome by diligent effort; but diligent effort can only be rightly directed and effectually employed as divine grace enables, and that grace is to be expectantly sought.

Probably it is best to begin by considering the fact of man's impotence. At first this may be presented in general terms and in its broad outlines by showing that the thrice holy God can require nothing less than holiness from His creatures, that He can by no means tolerate any sin in them. The standard which God has set before men is the moral law which demands perfect and perpetual obedience; being spiritual it enjoins holiness of character as well as conduct, purity of heart as well as acts. Such a standard fallen man cannot reach, such demands he cannot meet, as is demonstrated from the entire history of the Jews under that law.

Next it should be pointed out that the Lord Jesus did not lower that standard or modify God's commands, but uniformly and insistently upheld the one and pressed the other, as is unmistakably clear in Matthew 5:17-48; nevertheless He repeatedly affirmed the moral impotence of fallen man (John 5:44; 6:44; 8:43). This same twofold teaching is repeated by the apostles, especially in the epistles to the Romans and Corinthians.

From the general we may descend to the particular and show the extent of man's impotence and depravity. Sin has so ruined the whole of his being that the understanding is darkened, the heart corrupted, the will perverted, each detail being proved and illustrated from Scripture. Then in summing up this solemn aspect, appeal may be made to that word of Christ's where He declared not merely that there were many things (or even some things) man could not do without His enablement, but that without Him man could do nothing" (John 15:5)—nothing good, nothing acceptable to God. If man could prepare himself to turn to God, or turn of himself after the Holy Spirit has prepared him, he could do much. But since it is God who works in us "both to will and to do of his good pleasure" (Phil. 2:13), He is the One who first implants the desire and then gives the power to fulfill it. Not only must the understanding be so enlightened as to discern the good from the evil, but the heart has to be changed so as to prefer the good before the evil.

Next it is well to show clearly the nature of man's inability: what it does not consist of (the lack of faculties suited to the performance of duty) and what it does consist of. Care needs to be taken and arguments given to show that man's inability is moral rather than physical, voluntary rather than compulsory, criminal rather than innocent. After this has been done at some length, confirmation may be obtained by an appeal to the hearer's own experience. If honest he must acknowledge that his own consciousness testifies to the fact that he sins willingly and there-fore willfully, and that his conscience registers condemnation upon him. The very facts that we sin freely and that conscience accuses us show we ought to have avoided it. Whatever line a man takes in attempting to justify his own wrongdoing, he promptly forsakes it whenever his fellow-men wrong him. He never argues that they were unable to do otherwise, nor does he excuse them on the ground of their inheriting a corrupt nature from Adam! Moreover, in the hour of remorse, the man who has squandered his substance and wrecked his health does not even excuse himself, but freely owns "What a fool I have been! There is no one to blame but myself."

The impotence of the natural man to choose God for his portion is greater than that of an ape to reason like an Isaac Newton, yet there is this vital difference between the two: the inability of the former is a criminal one, that of the latter is not so because of its native and original incapacity. Man's moral inability lies not in the lack of capacity but in lack of desire. One incurs no guilt when there is a willingness of mind and a desire of heart to do the thing commanded but no capacity to carry it out. But where there is capacity (competent faculties) but unwilling-ness, there is guilt—wherever disaffection for God exists so does sin. Man's moral inability consists of an inveterate aversion for God, and it is this corruption of heart which alone has influence to prevent the proper use of the faculties with which he is endowed, and issues in acts of sin and rebellion against God. Even the bare knowledge of duty in all cases renders moral agents under obligation to do it: "To him that knoweth to do good, and doeth it not, to him it is sin" (Jam. 4:17).

It is very necessary that the preacher should be perfectly clear in his own mind that the moral impotence of the natural man is not of such a nature as to exempt him from God's claims or excuse him from the discharge of his duties. Some have drawn the erroneous conclusion that it is incongruous to call upon the unregenerate to perform spiritual duties. They say that only exhortations suited to the state of the unregenerate, such as the performance of civil righteousness, should be addressed to them. The truth is that a perfect heart and a perfect life are as much required as if men were not fallen creatures, and required of the greatest sinner as much as of the best saint. The righteous demands of the Most High must not be whittled down because of human depravity. David did not trim his exhortations to meet the inability of man: "Kiss the Son, lest he be angry, and ye perish from the way" (Ps. 2:12). Isaiah did not keep back the command "Wash you, make you clean; put away the evil of your doings from before mine eyes" (1:16) though he knew the people were so corrupt they would not and could not comply.

Urgent Invitation Obligatory

Nor should the preacher have the slightest hesitation in urging the unregenerate to use the means of grace and in declaring it is men's certain duty to employ them. The divine ordinances of hearing and reading the Word, of praying and conversing with God's people, are thereby made a real test of men's hearts—as to whether they really desire salvation or despise it. Though God does renew men by His Spirit, yet He appoints the means by which sinners are to be subservient to such a work of grace. If they scorn and neglect the means, the blame is in themselves and not in God. If we are not willing to seek salvation, it proves we have no desire to find it; then in the day to come we shall be reproved as wicked and slothful servants (Matt. 25:26). The plea that man has no power will then mean nothing, for then the fact that his lack of power consists only in a lack of heart will appear with sunlight clearness, and he will be justly condemned for contempt of God's Word; his blood will be upon his own head for disregarding the warnings of God's servants.

Yet so perverse is fallen human nature that men will argue, "What is the good of using the means when it does not lie in our power to give effect to them?" Even if there were no hope of success, God's command for us to use the means is sufficient to demand our compliance: "Master, we have toiled all the night, and have taken nothing: nevertheless at thy word I will let down the net" (Luke 5:5). I cannot infallibly promise a farmer who plows and sows that he will have a good crop, yet I may assure him that it is God's general way to bless the prudent and diligent. I cannot say to everyone who desires posterity, "Marry and you shall have children." But I may point out that if people refuse the ordinance of marriage they will never have any lawful children. The preacher needs to point out the grave peril incurred by those who spurn the help God proffers. Felix "trembled" (Acts 24:25), but he failed to act on his convictions. Unless the Lord is sought while He is "near" us (Isa. 55:6), He may finally abandon us. Every resistance to the impressions of the Spirit leaves the heart harder than it was before.

After all that has been said it is scarcely necessary for us to press upon the preacher the tremendous importance of this doctrine. It displays as no other the perfect consistency of divine justice and grace. It reveals to the believer that his infirmities and imperfections are not the comforting cover-up of guilt that he would like to think they are. All moral infirmity, all lack of perfect holiness, is entirely his own fault, for which he should be deeply humbled. It shows sinners that their perdition is really altogether of themselves, for they are unwilling to be made clean. The kindest thing we can do for them is to shatter their self-righteous hopes, to make them realize both their utter helplessness and their entire inexcusableness. The high demands of God are to be pressed upon them with the design of bringing them to cry to Him to graciously work in them that which He requires. Genuine conviction of sin consists in a thorough realization of responsibility and guilt, of our inability and dependence upon divine grace. Nothing is so well calculated to produce that conviction, under the Spirit's blessing, as the faithful preaching of this unpalatable truth.